THE KU KLUX KLAN

Printing Statement:

Due to the very old age and scarcity of this book,
many of the pages may be hard to read due to the
blurring of the original text, possible missing pages,
missing text and other issues boyond our control.

Because this is such an important and rare work, we
believe it is best to reproduce this book regardless of
its original condition.

Thank you for your understanding.

THE KU KLUX KLAN:
A Study of the American Mind

BY

JOHN MOFFATT MECKLIN, Ph.D.

Humanas actiones neque ridere, neque flere,
nec detestari, sed intelligere.

Spinoza.

FIRST PUBLISHED IN 1924

REISSUED, 1963, BY RUSSELL & RUSSELL, INC.

L. C. CATALOG CARD NO: 63—15172

PRINTED IN THE UNITED STATES OF AMERICA

To
PRESIDENT HOPKINS AND THE DARTMOUTH ALUMNI
WHOSE FRIENDLY AID DID MUCH
TO MAKE THIS STUDY
POSSIBLE

CONTENTS

THE KU KLUX KLAN

CHAPTER I

THE RISE OF THE INVISIBLE EMPIRE

IN 1873 the Ku Klux Klan, outside the South, was a synonym for the most sinister and dangerous forces in American life. In the North it was associated with clandestine murder and masked rebellion. Who then would have dared to prophesy that within less than half a century this secret, oath-bound order would be revived and spread to every section of the country? Such, however, is the fact. The modern Klan was organized by William J. Simmons in 1915, enjoyed a precarious existence for several years, suddenly assumed proportions of national importance in 1920, survived the attack of the powerful *New York World* and a searching investigation by a committee of Congress, and to-day boasts of a following that is numbered in hundreds of thousands, perhaps millions. The rise of the modern Klan is the most spectacular of all the social movements in American society since the close of the World War. It

is the object of this and the following chapter to
state briefly the main facts in the revival of the
so-called "Invisible Empire" of the Knights of
the Ku Klux Klan.

I

Colonel William Joseph Simmons, the founder
of the modern Klan, tells us that for twenty years
he had given thought to the creation of an order
standing for a comprehensive Americanism that
would blot out Mason and Dixon's Line. Fascinated as he was from boyhood by the romantic
story of the old Klan of Reconstruction days,
which is looked upon in the South as the savior
of Southern civilization, he called the new order
the Knights of the Ku Klux Klan. On October
16, 1915, Mr. Simmons, together with some thirty-
four friends, three of whom were bona fide members of the old Klan, met and signed a petition
for a charter. The charter was granted and on
Thanksgiving night, 1915, they gathered "under
a blazing, fiery torch" on the top of Stone Mountain, near Atlanta, and took the oath of allegiance to the Invisible Empire, Knights of the
Ku Klux Klan. "And thus," says Simmons in his

characteristic high-flown language, "on the mountain top that night at the midnight hour, while men braved the surging blasts of wild wintry winds and endured a temperature far below freezing [a *World* reporter was unkind enough to consult the weather bureau record for that night and found the minimum temperature to be only forty-five degrees], bathed in the sacred glow of the fiery cross, the Invisible Empire was called from its slumber of half a century to take up a new task and fulfil a new mission for humanity's good and to call back to mortal habitation the good angel of practical fraternity among men" (*The A B C of the Ku Klux Klan,* Ku Klux Klan Press, Atlanta, Georgia).

For five years the Klan seems to have passed an uneventful existence, spreading very slowly and making no great impression upon the country. By the early fall of 1918 it was organized in localities of the South, especially in Alabama and Georgia, the usual manifestation of its presence being the posting of warnings as in the Reconstruction days. In Mobile, Alabama, where a strike was threatened in the government shipyards, masked men leaped from their cars clad in the Klan regalia and forced the driver of a patrol wagon to surrender the strike leader who was then spirited away. In all these earlier appearances the Klan directed its activities against alien enemies and those accused of being disloyal, the idlers and slackers, strike leaders, and immoral women. Public sentiment, as in the case of the Mobile incident, seems to have supported the Klansmen, doubtless because most of them represented the better element of the communities. There were sporadic references to the Klan during 1919 and the first half of 1920. But by the fall of 1920 the Klan showed a decided increase in its activities. Rumors arose that the Klan was gaining a foothold in the North. The National Association for the Advancement of Colored People sought to check its spread by asking Postmaster General Burleson to forbid the Klan the use of the mails. The Klan had, indeed, gained a foothold in New York though its movements were much hampered by the opposition of the police.

II

The rapid expansion of the order was due to a radical change in its organization in June, 1920. Imperial Wizard Simmons had proven himself to be a capable "spellbinder" but an impractical

dreamer with little organizing ability. His society was in financial straits. At most it numbered only four or five thousand members and
was doomed to go the way, apparently, of countless other organizations of a similar nature. At
this juncture Mr. Edward Young Clarke and Mrs.
Elizabeth Tyler came to the aid of Wizard Simmons and his struggling society and rescued it
from oblivion. They had been associated for
years in connection with the Southern Publicity
Association and had been successful in drives for
funds for such organizations as the Anti-Saloon
League, the Roosevelt Memorial Fund, the Near-
East Relief, and similar movements. They lis-
tened to the schemes of Simmons and thought
they saw in the Klan financial possibilities. A
contract was entered into by which Clarke became
head of the propaganda department with complete charge of organization. Aided by Mrs.
Tyler, whose gifts as an organizer and promoter
he asserted were second only to his own, they pro-
ceeded to "sell" the Klan to the American public.

Within a little over a year, that is, in the period
between June, 1920, when the contract was entered upon, and October, 1921, when the Klan was
investigated by Congress, the Klan had grown

from a few thousand to something like 100,000
members. Clarke, aided by Mrs. Tyler, had applied to Klan promotion the skill acquired
through long experience. The country was divided into some eight or more "domains," or
geographical areas, such as Southeast, Southwest,
Northeast, the Mississippi Valley, the Pacific
Coast. Each "domain" was divided into
"realms," or states. The head of the promotion
department as a whole was Imperial Kleagle
E. Y. Clarke. The head of the "domain" was
called a Grand Goblin. The head of the "realm,"
or state, was called a King Kleagle, and the house-
to-house solicitors, or legwork men, were called
Kleagles. There can be little doubt that the
purely commercial motive had much to do with
the successful promotion of the Klan. The membership fee was ten dollars, which was divided
as follows: four of the ten dollars went to the
Kleagle, or local solicitor, when he signed up a
new member; one dollar went into the pocket of
the King Kleagle, or state sales-manager; the
Grand Goblin, or district salesman, had to be content with only fifty cents, while the remaining
four dollars and fifty cents went to Atlanta. It
will be seen that the inducement to the solicitor
was liberal. The purely commercial element has,

however, been overemphasized. It plays a part naturally and inevitably in every such system of promotion. But it must not be forgotten that the commercial motive alone can never explain the marvellous spread of the Klan.

This period of remarkable expansion was accompanied by a wave of lawlessness and crime which, rightly or wrongly, was associated with the Ku Klux Klan. From October, 1920, to October, 1921, the *New York World* reported four killings, one mutilation, one branding with acid, forty-one floggings, twenty-seven tar and feather parties, five kidnappings, forty-three individuals warned to leave town or otherwise threatened, fourteen communities threatened by posters, sixteen parades of masked men with warning placards. These outbreaks were characterized, generally, by two peculiarities. They were "punishments" administered to individuals because of alleged violation of statute law or of the demands of good morals and they were committed after nightfall by parties whose identity was concealed by masks. The name of the Ku Klux Klan was very generally associated by the public with these outrages. The *New York World* and many other papers asserted that for all these outrages the Klan was either directly or indirectly responsible. Emperor Sim-

mons as emphatically denied that the official Klan
had anything to do with them. What is of more
immediate concern to us in this connection is that
these outrages were directly responsible for the
exposure by the *New York World* and the Congressional investigation of October, 1921.

III

The investigation of the *New York World,* in
view of the strict secrecy of the Klan and the fact
that the investigators did not have power of sub-
pœna and were forced to deal with rumor and
voluntary information, is little short of a master-
piece of newspaper efficiency. It indicates con-
vincingly that it is impossible for any organization claiming to be secret and yet dealing with
matters of public import to conceal its inner
workings from the public. There is no doubt that
these *World* investigators were better posted as
to the work of the Klan than were individual
Klansmen themselves. It is probable, also, that
the government secret service accumulated information fully as complete as that of the *World*
and is well posted on the activities of the Klan.
These facts should put a crimp in the self-
confidence of any organization attempting to

defy public opinion and operate in the dark. It should convince secret orders of every variety that in a free country secrecy is tolerated not because the public cannot help itself but because the authorities of the state look upon such secrecy as harmless. In no other nation in the world is public curiosity keener or the machinery for gratifying that curiosity developed to such perfection. The moral of all this is that it is the part of wisdom to do all things of real importance for public welfare openly and above board. Any other course must inevitably subject the order concerned to the humiliation of having its secrets aired in hostile fashion in public. The officials of the Klan complained bitterly that the *World* was brutally inconsiderate when it published the Klan ritual, held up to ridicule its bombastic rhetoric, its outlandish nomenclature, and its childish mummeries. The reply is that the Klan challenged just such an exposure when it boasted of its impenetrable secrecy. Its hood and gown, its ghostly parades, its anonymous threats, its boast of an Invisible Empire that "sees all and hears all" were a direct challenge to the press to find out the truth. If any Klansmen of finer sensibilities, and there are many such, were mortified by the sorry figures cut by Emperor Simmons,

Imperial Kleagle Clarke, and Mrs. Tyler when exposed to the light of publicity, they have only themselves and the policy of their order to thank for it.

It was undoubtedly the conviction of the *World* that a thoroughgoing exposure of the secrets of the Klan and a scathing arraignment of its methods would suffice to discredit it with the American people. In its arraignment of the Klan, however, it is a question whether this great daily did not overshoot the mark and defeat its own ends. The *World* overestimated the number and power of the Klan, for it talked of a membership of 500,000, and even of 700,000, when Congressional investigation showed that the Klan in October, 1921, numbered hardly more than 100,000. The *World* ascribed the success of the Klan to a skilful salesmanship of hate in that it resorted "to every 'wrinkle' which practical salesmanagership keeps in its box of tricks" to make effective its appeal "to the ignorant, the cruel, the cowardly, and the vengeful." But to assume that the remarkable spread of the Klan was due solely or mainly to its appeal to base and selfish motives is misleading. In this vast movement, becoming cumbersome in its purposeless opportunism and swelling to hundreds of thousands during 1921 and 1922, many elements entered. A most important factor was unquestionably the system of salesmanship initiated by E. Y. Clarke. Even granting, however, that Clarke and his assistants were merely commercializing hates and prejudices, it is well to remember that men joined the Klan because it appealed to their patriotism and their moral idealism more than to their hates and prejudices. The baser motives were present, but they alone can never account for the spread of the Klan.

Perhaps the fundamental mistake of the newspapers is that they failed to grasp the Klan's real significance. The *World* described the Klan as something alien to American life, a cancer eating its way into the vitals of society. The Klan is painted as thoroughly un-American. The Klan, with equal confidence, asserts that it stands for "one hundred percent Americanism." If the Klan were utterly un-American it could never have succeeded as it has. The Klan is not alien to American society. If it were, the problem would be much simpler. The Klan is but the recrudescence of forces that already existed in American society, some of them recent, others dating from the more distant past. It gives a totally false idea of the social significance of the

Klan, therefore, to liken it, as does the *World,* to an alien and destructive force "tunneling, mole-like, under the whole structure of American institutions." It is the object of this study to show that the Klan draws its inspirations from ancient prejudices, classical hatreds, and ingrained social habits. The germs of the disease of the Klan, like germs in the human body, have long been present in the social organism and needed only the weakening of the social tissue to become malignant.

The hope that publication of the facts would kill the Klan has not been realized. The *World's* exposure was published in eighteen leading dailies, including such Southern papers as the *New Orleans Times-Picayune, Houston Chronicle, Dallas News, Galveston News, Columbus* (Ga.) *Enquirer-Sun,* and the *Oklahoman.* But since the *World's* exposure and the Congressional investigation the Klan has flourished like a green bay tree and to-day numbers hundreds of thousands, possibly millions. Here is matter for reflection for every one interested in the workings of the American mind and the part played by the press in the formation of public sentiment. It suggests that something more is needed than the mere publication of the facts. There is necessary, for effective public opinion, a critical and impartial weighing of those facts, an interpretation of their meaning which will enable men to arrive at the truth. It is almost impossible, it seems, for the newspaper reporter to resist the temptation either to play the prosecuting attorney or to cast his facts in a "story" form, thereby running the danger of perverting their meaning. The "story" of the *World* reporters is interesting but not convincing. With the best of intentions the *World* has hardly given us an unbiased and critical estimate of the significance of the Klan. What the press exposure and the Congressional investigation did give to the Klan was a vast amount of gratuitous and invaluable advertising. The moral of it all seems to be that there is a crying need for some group or some social organ which can take the facts presented by the press or federal investigators and interpret them to the masses of Americans. What impresses the student of the Klan movement at every stage is the lack, on the part of the average American, of any real insight into its significance. Not man's innate depravity, not overt criminal acts, nor yet wicked attempts to subvert American institutions, but rather plain old-fashioned ignorance is the real enemy of that huge giant, the public, who is the fumbling physician of our social ills.

IV

There are at least three possible estimates of
Emperor Simmons, the founder and in many ways
the most interesting figure in the Klan movement.
The first, and perhaps the most charitable, is that
he is a well-meaning dreamer, impractical and in-
efficient, however, in business matters, and that
he was imposed upon by Clarke and his lieuten-
ants, who sought to commercialize the Klan. A
second and quite opposite estimate is that of Cap-
tain Fry, former Kleagle of the Klan, who later
resigned and served as one of the chief sources
of the information of the *World*. (Mr. Fry has
published this information in book form under the
title *The Modern Ku Klux Klan*.) Emperor Simmons, according to Mr. Fry, is "a cunning, shrewd
adventurer, who from the start conceived the idea
of acquiring both wealth and unlimited power
through his secret 'Invisible Empire.' In all his
public utterances, in the newspapers and before
Congress, he has shown a shiftiness and evasive-
ness clearly discernible amidst a vast mass of
wordiness." A third explanation is that Emperor
Simmons started out to organize a purely fraternal and patriotic society. He did not make a
success of it, and Clarke and Tyler showed him

how to turn the trick by exploiting the hates and prejudices rampant in the post-war period. Simmons was so carried away with their immediate success that he sanctioned their methods tacitly, if not openly. Our final pronouncement upon the character of the man must be conditioned by some insight into the workings of his mind.

To judge by the external appearance of this tall, thin-lipped, bespectacled Southerner with his rather tense and emotional expression one might easily classify him as a revivalist preacher or a political "spellbinder" of the familiar Southern type. As a matter of fact he has been a preacher, a travelling salesman, a promoter of fraternal organizations, and a professor of Southern history in a Southern institution. The man reflects his background in thought and act, for he fairly exudes uncritical sentimentalism of the conventional type. Emperor Simmons is a dreamer, even a mystic, with considerable oratorical power. His habits of thought are those of the emotional preacher of limited education accustomed to appeal to the feelings and the imagination rather than to reason. He is, above all, keenly, almost intuitively, alert to the feelings of the average man. Reading his public utterances, one gets the impression of a man whose temperament and training are inimical to strict intellectual integrity. One feels that without any conscious departure from the truth he could very easily convince himself, under the pressure of the immediate situation, that the particular point he wished to make was the whole truth and nothing but the truth. This is important if we are to understand the success of the chief evangelist of that tangled mass of half-truths, passionate loyalties, traditional prejudices, and unreasoned convictions that go to make up the Klan gospel.

Simmons is not a genius in any sense of the term. He failed signally as a practical organizer. Neither in his public utterances nor in the Klan literature that comes from his pen do we find great or original ideas. He does possess, however, a singular ability to insinuate himself into the sympathies of the average man of the middle class and to play upon his likes and dislikes. In this respect Simmons has served as the model for all Klan leaders and organizers. This is perhaps his most important contribution to the Klan movement. It was by mere chance that his Klan idea fell upon the fruitful soil of the troubled post-war period, was capitalized and "sold" by Clarke and Tyler, and, as it gained headway, gathered to itself a hodgepodge of forces racial, religious, patriotic,

political, and moral, precipitated by the turmoil of
war and awaiting some means of crystallization
and direction.   Emperor Simmons and his Klan
are more or less historical accidents.

The official Klan literature from the pen of Emperor Simmons faithfully reflects the mental attitudes of the group he represents.   It is conventionally and uncritically patriotic.   The ritual of
the Klan, called the Kloran, copyrighted in 1916
by W. J. Simmons of Atlanta, Georgia, and ac-
cessible on the shelves of the Library of Congress,
abounds in asseverations of one hundred percent
Americanism.   The ritual is not characterized by
great beauty or dignity and is conventionally religious.   The orthodox tenets of Evangelicalism
from the Blood Atonement to Verbal Inspiration
are all there, by implication at least.   A Fundamentalist would certainly find himself thoroughly
at home in the atmosphere of the Klan cere-
monies.   The writer does not find any justification, however, for the charge of the *World* reporter that the Klan ritual makes a sacrilegious
use of the rite of baptism.   Three of the nine
questions put to the Klan candidate reflect the
ideals of the middle-class, hundred-percent Americanism to which the Klan makes its appeal.   The
first question, ''Are you a native-born American

citizen?" excludes the foreigner. The third question, "Do you believe in the tenets of the Christian religion?" is intended to exclude the Jew, though it might be answered in the affirmative by the liberal Jew who identified the "tenets of the Christian religion" with the utterances of the great Jew, Jesus of Nazareth, rather than with the dogmas of Evangelicalism derived from John Calvin or Wesley. This leads one to suspect that the real grounds for excluding the Jew are other than those of creed. The fifth question, "Do you believe in the distinctive institutions of our civil government and the constitutional rights of free speech, free public schools, free press, and the separation of church and state?" is obviously aimed at the Catholic. There is nothing in the Klan's ritual or constitution that would subject it to criticism. Its official documents indicate in perfectly clear language that the Klan originally, no matter what it later became in actual practice, was a purely fraternal and patriotic organization, one of hundreds of similar secret societies in this country.

V

The Congressional investigation of October, 1921, is in many respects the climax of the dramatic evolution of the modern Ku Klux Klan. It is a climax in which the melodramatic, not to say the comic, elements far outweigh the tragic, and the chief actor was Emperor Simmons. He played his part well. The Hon. William Jennings Bryan, who seems to be spending his declining days tilting at theological windmills, is accustomed to set his anti-evolutionist audiences in a roar by crying, "You can't make a monkey of me." Emperor Simmons, an ardent follower of Bryan and the Fundamentalists, likewise refused to permit the hostile committee of Congress to make a monkey of him. Armed with unfailing good humor, an unlimited supply of spellbinding rhetoric, perfect self-possession, and a ready and specious reply to every question, Emperor Simmons foiled every effort of the gentlemen of the committee, the most of whom were distinctly hostile, to connect the official Klan with the various outrages attributed to it by the press and public. After a candid reading of the report of the investigations of the Klan by the House Rules Committee of Congress one is inclined to say "not proven." No ground for federal action against the Klan was established.

Inconclusive as were the results of this investigation, so far as either condemning or exonerating

the Klan is concerned, they throw a most interesting light upon the head of the Klan and the
relations of the official to the local Klans. To the
question of Representative Fess, ''Is the purpose
of this order anything like that of the Invisible
Empire in Civil War times?'' Emperor Simmons
replied without the least hesitation, ''No, sir; we
have no conditions existing now that would justify
such a modus operandi. This is purely a fraternal and patriotic organization and is in no
sense a regulative or corrective organization.''
How Emperor Simmons reconciles this statement
with his other public utterances and with the
lengthy and grandiloquent first degree of the
Kloran given to all initiates into the Klan, in
which the old Klan is glorified and emphasis is
laid upon the fact that the modern Klan is a con-
tinuation of the Klan of Reconstruction days, it
is difficult to decide. Simmons was doubtless not
guilty of conscious duplicity. Before the House
Committee he had a case to make out. He had to
convince these gentlemen and the listening public
that the Klan was not open to criminal prosecution. He took as his text the principles laid down
in the early literature of the Klan long before the
''salesmen of hate,'' E. Y. Clarke and Mrs. Eliza-

beth Tyler, had inaugurated a period of unprecedented expansion.

With this object in view it was perfectly possible
for a man of Simmons's temperament to convince
himself of the justice of his position. Officially
the Klan was and still remains a purely fraternal
and patriotic organization. Officially the Klan is
opposed to profiteering in race prejudice and
religious bigotry. Officially the Klan does not
sanction the assumption either by individuals or
local Klans of the rôle of regulators of public
morals and the enforcement of law. Officially the
Klan is supposed never to act in its corporate
capacity except when assembled in its local
Klavern. Technically the position of Emperor
Simmons was correct. But abundant data are at
hand which indicate that in actual practice in the
various communities the local Klan is something
quite different. The parades, the anonymous
threatening letters, the whippings, the tar and
feather parties, the political programs in states
such as Oregon and Texas, the appearance
of masked men in churches to make donations to
weak-kneed preachers—these and countless other
activities disprove the Emperor's contention that

would," as he remarks in another connection, "have tucked up our great, long, forked tail, folded our horns, and taken to the tall timber."

In his effort to convince the Committee of the inherent humility of his soul Emperor Simmons grows more intimate and says: "My disposition from boyhood has been tinged with a distinctive streak of timidity and I have never had any desire to rule or govern." He never goes to meetings, he asserts, "without a vivid consciousness of my unworthiness, and my desire to be down the line sitting in the chairs with the other fellows." We fear the Emperor does himself injustice, for there is certainly nothing to indicate such shrinking modesty in his record before the hostile and powerful Congressional Committee where he bears himself with the unruffled good humor and perfect ease of a veteran. Most unpleasant of all to this lover of democratic simplicity is the insinuation that he is adopting the habits of a luxury-loving despot. "Only yesterday I read in the paper, sir, that I appeared before your honorable committee with a great diamond pin in my tie." The Emperor hastens to disabuse the public of such a monstrous misapprehension. "That is no diamond," he says; "that is an imperial stone."

The penumbra of vagueness, that characterizes

the thinking of Simmons and makes futile any attempt to give clear and final formulation to the Klan ideals, appears in his reply to the charge that the emphasis on white supremacy "is being taken as an indication that the organization has for its mission the practice of violence and injustice towards other races and colors." Simmons's reply is: "That is not so. The supremacy of the white man means the supremacy of the white man's mind as evidenced by the achievements of our civilization." The Klan's object is "to preserve the dignity and achievements of the white race in justice, fairness, and equity toward all the human family." To identify "white supremacy" with the "supremacy of the white man's mind" is to talk a language that the average Klansman could not understand, and it gives to the phrase a twist which, to say the least, is totally foreign to its accepted meaning. It must be remembered, however, that Emperor Simmons's immediate problem when asked this question before a committee of Congress was to offer a definition of "white supremacy" that would pass muster with the Fourteenth and Fifteenth amendments and the Bill of Rights.

In reply to the suggestion that the Klan organizers were obtaining members through the circulation of anti-Catholic literature, Emperor Simmons states: "I will say to you in all frankness that there was only one instance according to my recollection where a Kleagle circulated or attempted to circulate anti-Catholic literature, and within less than a week, as soon as I could get at that man, he was forever discharged from our work and for that reason." This is, in truth, an astonishing statement, for it is the writer's opinion, based upon a perusal of Klan literature, the replies to numerous letters, and first-hand knowledge of the Klan in various sections of the country, that the Klan's anti-Catholic propaganda has won for it more members than anything else. To this statement must be added what Simmons says in regard to the mask: "Are we the only people that use a mask? If so, what about Mardi Gras celebrations in this country, and what about Hallowe'en celebrations? . . . Our mask and robe, I say before God, are as innocent as the breath of an angel." The parades were "never for the purpose of intimidation."

Towards the close of the investigation Chairman Campbell asked: "Has it occurred to you that this idealistic organization that you have given birth to and have fostered so long is now being used for mercenary purposes by very clever

people or propagandists who know how to appeal
to people in this community or that for membership?" To this Simmons replied: "Nothing has
come to my view that would prompt me to have
such an opinion." Thus was the issue made up
between Emperor Simmons and the Committee of
Congress. Simmons insisted that the real Klan
was the Klan as he originally conceived it and as
he formulated its ideals in the early Klan literature. He carefully sought to divorce from the
official Klan of which he was the head every alleged
outrage, even in such cases as that of Beaumont,
Texas, where the local Klan assumed responsibility for its acts. The veil of secrecy that sepa-
rates local Klans from each other and even from
the central Klan authorities enabled Emperor
Simmons to make out his case, for when he insisted that the official Klan was not responsible
for these local outrages the committee was forced
to take his word.

This brings us, then, to the ultimate question,
What is the real Klan? Is it the Klan as described by Emperor Simmons before Congress or
is it the local Klan active in Beaumont, Texas;
Mer Rouge, Louisiana; Portland, Oregon? Does
Simmons's assertion that the Klan is "a purely
fraternal and patriotic organization and is in no

sense a regulative and corrective organization''
give us the real Klan or are we to find it in the
numerous statements in the public press telling of
the "strong arm" methods of the Klan in its attempts to "clean up" the various communities
and its strenuous efforts after political power in
city, state, and nation? From what does the
Klan draw its vitality? Does it owe its power to
its loyalty to the amiable, innocuous and thoroughly conventional ideals of the official Klan
documents or does it secure it through a clever
appeal to the prejudices of well-intentioned people? Does the real Klan speak through the high-
flown rhetoric and irreproachable ethics of Simmons before the Committee of Congress or
through the shrieking Klan publications, such as
*The Searchlight, Sgt. Dalton's Weekly, The Fiery
Torch?* The facts seem to indicate that the Klan
of Emperor Simmons is a pure idealization and
to all intents and purposes non-existent. (The
real Klan is the *local* organization, which, owing
primarily to its secrecy, is a law unto itself.)

CHAPTER II

THE RISE OF THE INVISIBLE EMPIRE
(*Continued*)

I

AFTER the Congressional investigations in October, 1921, the Klan spread with amazing rapidity. The center of the Klan's strength was not at first and never has been in the older South. It was in the great area west of the Mississippi that includes northern and eastern Texas, Arkansas, Oklahoma, and northern Louisiana, a region which was singularly adapted to the spread of Klan ideas, that the Klan reached its first peak of success. It was early transplanted to the Pacific coast, finding ready followers in the Sacramento Valley and southern California. From California the Klan was introduced into Oregon where it soon became a factor of prime importance in the affairs of that state. More recently the Klan has met with astonishing success in the Middle West. It is quite possible that at present the Klan has in the two states of Ohio and Indiana over half a

31

million followers, or more than in all the southern states east of the Mississippi. At present the Klan is showing considerable activity in the neighborhood of New York City, which may indicate an attempt to storm this stronghold of all those things to which the Klan stands opposed.

Any attempt to estimate the actual membership of a secret order of such mushroom growth as the Klan must of course be largely a matter of guess. A recent investigator puts the total membership at two and one half millions. (Robert L. Duffus, "The Ku Klux Klan in the Middle West," *World's Work*, July, 1923.) This seems a rather liberal estimate. But if we include in that number those who have resigned from the Klan, cases of which the present writer has found in every community where the Klan is active, members who are only nominally connected with the order, and a rather nondescript group of Klan sympathizers who on occasion may lend their support to the Klan, it is possible to place the estimate of the Klan following at between two and three millions. This is indeed a formidable figure and were the Klan more closely organized and animated by a more definite and comprehensive program it might become a force to be reckoned with in national life. There is, however, little danger that the Klan as a whole will ever be able to utilize all its strength in a political or social program. This is due to the essentially local nature of the Klan, its singular lack of able and statesmanlike leaders, its planless opportunism, and, above all, its dearth of great unifying and constructive ideals. In the language of Freudianism, the Klan is essentially a defense mechanism against evils which are often more imaginary than real. It is for this reason negative rather than constructive in its influence.

II

There is the greatest variety of attitudes towards the Klan in the various sections of the country and even within each state, indicating the chaotic condition of public sentiment with regard to the movement. A typical Middle Western attitude is expressed by a citizen of Kansas City, Missouri: "Minority favorable among the Protestants. Catholics antagonistic. Dominant sentiment probably unfavorable on the ground that the Klan movement is unwholesome in its secrecy and in arousing antagonisms." Among the rather phlegmatic and free-thinking German population of Davenport, Iowa, one finds a feeling of "amused tolerance." In the Middle West, the stronghold of the A. P. A. (American Protective Association) movement in the nineties, anti-Catholicism seems to take precedence over everything else. A statement from Topeka, Kansas, is significant: "As near as we know the foundation of Klanism here is fear and suspicion of the Roman Catholic Church." The writer, Meredith Nicholson, of Indianapolis, states: "In Indiana the movement seems to be almost wholly anti-Catholic." An intelligent Klansman from Chicago gives as the chief sources of Klan support in that city "the bitter opposition to the Hearst newspapers and the hostility to those who stand for ecclesiastical autocracy and Romanistic influence upon the American government and its public officials—probably more joining it for this reason than for any other. The open opposition of Catholics and Jews in politics is helping the movement to a great extent." On the other hand, the editor of the *Chicago Defender,* who belongs to a group whose more intelligent members have shown a keen appreciation of the meaning of the Klan movement, namely, the Negroes, probably describes the feeling in the large city towards the Klan when he says: "The general attitude in this community [Chicago] is hostile because of the existence of a large foreign population and large numbers of the followers of the Roman Catholic faith and strong labor organizations. All these elements represent considerable political strength. Our recent Republican candidate for Mayor, accused of having the support of the Ku Klux Klan interests, was decisively defeated by the Democratic candidate whose religion is Catholic and who received the full support of the powerful Negro vote."

It is a great mistake to imagine that the Klan dominates the South. Even in states such as Texas, where the Klan is supposed to be strong, there is, in every community, an intelligent and influential group opposed to the Klan. A citizen of Houston says: "The good attained has been more than counterbalanced by the ill-feeling created and the many instances in which injustice has been done." A correspondent from Austin asserts: "The Klan is a disturbing force, causing animosities to supplant the ordinary civilities and harmony that prevailed before." A Galveston editor thinks: "The general attitude of the community is unfavorable to the Klan. This is true because of the cosmopolitan nature of the population, including many foreign-born, descendants of foreign-born, a goodly number of Catholic and Jewish residents and a large percentage of native-born Americans who have travelled and who have some breadth of vision." In Oklahoma, in many ways the paradise of the Klan, the attitude is "favorable among Protestants on the whole." A minister of Lake Charles, southern Louisiana, thus described conditions there during the Mer Rouge murder trials: "Political and business animosities are being aroused. Men talk fight. One old-timer said yesterday, 'If they are going to fight let's have it out now and not leave it to our children.' He is a Catholic and an old-time gunman but at present a fine citizen."

In the older sections of the South statements vary from "indifferent" or even "amused tolerance" in the settled communities of the Carolinas and Virginia and in Savannah, Georgia, to "favorable" and "good-naturedly tolerant" in communities such as Atlanta and Birmingham, where the Klan is strong. There is pronounced antagonism in cosmopolitan cities such as New Orleans. In Atlanta, the home of the Klan, formidable opposition is quietly taking shape under the leadership of prominent pastors of the city. Curious to relate, the state that was the hot-bed of Reconstruction and old Klan activities, South Carolina, is one of the states least affected by the modern Klan. A prominent citizen of Columbia, where the carpet-bag legislature sat in all its sable glory in 1870, states: "The Ku Klux Klan is not in evidence in our section. . . . I hear little about them and I think the sentiment is generally against them." Reports from other sections of the state are "little interest," "interest sporadic," "hardly ever hear the Klan discussed."

Summarizing our data, we may conclude that, where the Klan is not active, the general opinion, based upon newspaper reports and more or less calm and impersonal judgment, is uniformly unfavorable. Where the Klan secures a foothold in the community and makes itself felt, as is often the case, in the rôle of moral reformer, unearthing the bootlegger or chastising criminals and disreputable characters that have escaped the law, the judgment is sometimes favorable. In communities where the Klan gets to be a power, where its secret hand is felt in business, politics, social and religious relations, there is always a strong, often bitter, undercurrent of anti-Klan sentiment. The best citizens oppose it because it breeds social discord. But it is important to note that in almost every case this feeling is expressed with caution, the individual often not wishing to be quoted. The Klan is openly challenged by a few courageous individuals only. The rank and

file even of the better citizens who do not approve
of the Klan keep quiet from prudential motives.   Here we have the insidious influence of
a powerful secret order in stifling public sentiment.

III

A canvass of the motives for joining the Klan
indicates that anti-Catholicism takes precedence
over all others.   Other incentives, to be sure, are
mentioned, such as one hundred percent Americanism, law and order, anti-Semitism, white supremacy, and the purity of womanhood.   But
neither anti-Catholicism nor the other motives
mentioned for supporting the Klan represent
reasoned convictions.   They are vague phrases
symbolizing "sets" in the emotional life, conventional loyalties, unreasoned prejudices, or fixed
ideas which the individual would be sadly non-
plussed to justify critically.   They serve a useful
purpose, perhaps, in that they enable groups and
communities to introduce some sort of unity into
thought and life.   Critical reflection plays a
very small part in the situation.   The average
man acquires his traditional mental attitudes,
such as a prejudice against the Pope, not from

any first-hand information about this i
but primarily through the impact of the
ing uncritical Protestant antipathies to 1
It is primarily because of the absence o
and independent thinking in these mat
the Klan is enabled to exploit these traditional
loyalties in its own interest.

While anti-Catholicism bulks largest in Klan objectives it would be a mistake to suppose that anti-Catholicism, anti-Semitism, white supremacy, or one hundred percent Americanism occupied a prominent position at the inception of the modern Klan. As already indicated, the Klan at first was a "purely fraternal and patriotic organization." It may be seriously doubted whether its founder ever intended at first that the Klan should play the rôle of reformer, seek to check the spread of the Catholic Church, or pose as the champion of the white race. In fact, the incentives used to gain members for the Klan have varied with the different stages of the Klan's evolution. At the time of its inception, if we may trust the word of Emperor Simmons, the appeal of the Klan was intended to be that of a secret fraternal and patriotic organization drawing romantic inspiration from the old Ku Klux Klan, an appeal which, judging from the success of the

Klan from 1915 to 1920, was not very effective. But even during this early period, as indicated by the occasional newspaper references to the Klan's activities, it is probable that the rôle of a vigilance committee rather than that of a purely fraternal order was the real attraction of the Klan. The traditions of the old Klan together with the lax post-war conditions acted to combine to turn the Klan into a sort of local hooded vigilantes.

Through its stand for law and order the Klan gained the support of many of the best citizens made uneasy by the lawlessness of post-war days. In Houston, Texas, for example, there had been serious trouble with the Negro soldiery during the war. The Klan organizer played upon the fear born of this unpleasant experience to induce many of the leading citizens of Houston to join the Klan as a means of protecting the whites against possible outbreaks by the returned Negro soldiery. The writer was informed by a member of the famous Morehouse Klan of Louisiana that long before the Klan appeared in that community the leading citizens had organized a "Law and Order League" to correct the intolerable conditions that followed the war. When the Klan organizers appeared these men identified themselves

with it for the same reason that they had formed
their "Law and Order League." In almost every
instance where the Klan is defended it is because
of its efforts at local reform. Invariably, when
newly organized Klans asked the Atlanta authorities what to do, the reply was to "clean up" the
community, no matter whether that community
was New York City or Trinidad, Colorado. Here,
then, we have in the Klan's stand for law and
order its earliest effective justification for its existence, but a justification apparently never contemplated at the time of its organization.

Obviously, however, the work of a vigilance
committee is occasional and can only be justified
where abnormal conditions exist. It offers no
permanent basis for the life of an organization.
To survive, the Klan had to find some more effective appeal to the imaginations of men. When
E. Y. Clarke and Mrs. Tyler, the real creators of
the modern Klan, appeared upon the scene they
were faced with this practical problem of finding
something that would "sell." With the instinct
of practical salesmen they speedily discovered the
possibilities that lay in the traditional hates and
group prejudices that had been rubbed raw by the
friction of a great war. Operating in Georgia,
the state that had sent Thomas Watson, the arch

Catholic-baiter, to the Senate, that had experienced a wave of anti-Semitism in connection with the trial of the Jew, Frank, and that had led the Union in lynchings of Negroes, it is not surprising that these "salesmen of hate" speedily found that there were immense profits in purveying at ten dollars per initiate, anti-Catholicism, anti-Semitism and white supremacy, together with the more or less sentimental bargain-counter attractions of one hundred percent Americanism and the purity of womanhood. With its appeal to anti-Catholicism, for example, the Klan tapped at once a great stream of religious feeling that finds its fountain head in the fires of Smithfield and the Spanish Armada.' The Klan thereby made connection with that powerful body of middle class Protestant traditions which have registered themselves in the Know-Nothing Party of the middle of the last century and in the A. P. A. movement towards its close.

The final stage in the evolution of Klan objectives is reached when the Klan enters politics, a stage which seems to be more or less inevitable for the reason that in this country all movements of engrossing social significance sooner or later take on a political tinge. In a democracy it would appear that great social issues can only be solved in the political arena. In some cases, as in Oregon and Oklahoma, the Klan was forced into politics because the arm of the state was being used against it. It is obvious that when the Klan enters the political field it must tend to become but another political machine. This means the inevitable loss of whatever moral or idealistic appeal it may have enjoyed. It is then thrown back upon the brute strength of its organization and the political skill of its leaders. Its career must from the very nature of the case be brief and end in defeat and disintegration. The issues that have given the Klan its vitality do not lend themselves to political success, as is amply shown in the history of the Know-Nothings and of the A. P. A. movement.

IV

The story of the growth of the Klan in Oregon is most enlightening as illustrating Klan methods and suggesting what may be the future of the Klan movement. The Klan in Oregon is an importation from California and was organized in Medford, Jackson County, January, 1921. The enforcement of the prohibition law against the boot-leggers was then a live issue in the county,

and many joined the Klan for the avowed purpose
of assisting the officers of the law. Racial and religious antagonisms seem to have played no part
at the birth of the Klan in Oregon. In a state
where eighty-five percent of its people is native
white, three percent Negroes, five percent Orien-
tals, and less than eight percent Catholic, it would
appear that there was a complete lack of all those
things upon which the Klan was accustomed to
thrive. Yet the Klan grew rapidly. Here, as in
the case of the parent Klan at Atlanta, it appears
that clever "salesmanship" had much to do with
the rapidity of its growth. Grand Dragon Fred
L. Gifford, L. I. Powell, H. E. Griffith, and others,
proved themselves to be leaders of more than
usual ability. This hardly suffices, however, to
explain the astonishing readiness with which the
people of Oregon, only one and one-half percent
of whom are illiterate, swallowed the Klan doctrines.

The bulk of the people of Oregon came from
the great central Mississippi Valley. The recent
picturization of Emerson Hough's story, *The
Covered Wagon,* shows the long and painful
journey of the early pioneers from Missouri
across the desert to the green valleys of the
Pacific slope where their descendants now live.

They belong, therefore, to that old American stock from which throughout the Middle West the anti-Catholic and native American movements, the Know-Nothingism and the A. P. A., drew their chief support. Their mental attitudes, in spite of their freer western life, are not essentially different from those of the people of Texas, Missouri, Kansas, and Indiana. The anti-Catholic tradition has been generally familiar to them from childhood. Furthermore, these people settled in a state that consists of a vast central area of mountains and alkaline desert fringed on the north and west by narrow and fertile valleys There are few great trunk lines and it is easy to imagine that social traditions would remain largely unchallenged, in spite of an admirable educational system, in these narrow and shut-in valleys. It was throughout this region, at least, that the Klan spread with amazing rapidity and apparently without being challenged. Within a year there were few communities that did not have a Klan organization.

In a community congenial to Klan ideas and providing able leaders and organizers, it was inevitable that the Klan should get into politics. Two things seem to have hastened the coming of the political stage in the evolution of the Klan

in Oregon, namely, the political ambitions of the
Klan leaders and the proclamation of Governor
Olcott on May 13, 1922, condemning the Klan because of its alleged connection with night-riding
outrages in Medford and other places. This
proclamation precipitated a bitter political fight
in which Governor Olcott lost his office, the Klan
using its influence to secure the election of the
Democratic candidate, Walter N. Pierce, besides
putting through the so-called "compulsory school
bill" aimed at the Catholic schools. While the
campaign for the school bill was primarily a fight
for political power, religious issues were drawn
into it. The Klan, to forward its political schemes,
made extended and unscrupulous appeals to the
traditional anti-Catholic prejudices of the people.
Governor Olcott, a Protestant, was referred to as
"a candidate whose every recent act has borne the
indelible stamp of the Catholic Pope in Rome."
They adopted the ancient ruse, practised in the
Know-Nothing and A. P. A. movements, of putting forward "escaped" nuns who toured the state
warning against the Catholic menace. In its effort to strengthen its political power the Klan
sought the aid of the women and Americans of
foreign birth, the auxiliary orders of the Ladies
of the Invisible Empire and the Royal Riders of

the Red Robe being organized for this purpose. The Klan, which apparently never numbered over a hundred thousand members in the state, achieved its success politically by securing either as members or else as sympathizers political leaders and men prominent in business and civic affairs, by occasional appeal to the boycott, by the use of affiliated organizations such as the Ladies of the Invisible Empire and the Royal Riders of the Red Robe, and above all by acting as a united and militant minority, the Klan "bloc."

There are indications that the people of Oregon are wearying of Klan rule and for reasons that are exceedingly suggestive to the student of the Klan movement. In the first place the inevitable repercussion of the Klan "compulsory school act" is already in evidence. This act compels every parent or guardian, with certain minor exceptions, to send all children under their care between eight and sixteen to the public school or "be guilty of a misdemeanor, and each day's failure to send such child to a public school shall constitute a separate offence." Though this measure was proposed by a Scottish Rites Mason it seems to have been drafted by Klansmen and put through by their support. Leading Masons have condemned it. The real offence of this bill, which does not become law until 1926, and even then must run the chances of being pronounced unconstitutional, lies in the fact that it was drafted and put through by an organization that is militantly and avowedly anti-Catholic and anti-Jew. That is to say, it was not based upon any calm and statesmanlike consideration of what was best educationally for all concerned, but was actuated primarily by religious animosity. This, not to mention other criticisms to which it is subject, discredits the bill with all good, liberal-minded citizens.

The difficulties encountered by the courts in their efforts to bring to justice the perpetrators of the "necktie parties" and other night-riding outrages in Jackson County are also opening the eyes of the people of Oregon to the menace of a secret and oath-bound organization when its influence extends to the witness stand and the jury-box. Finally, it is being discovered in cities such as Portland, Astoria, and Medford, where the Klan is strong, that the presence in the community of a secret order, bent upon its own political aggrandizement, is deadly poison to civic spirit and hence to social progress. Chambers of Commerce and even fraternal organizations are feeling the disruptive effect of the Klan. Neighborhood civic clubs are being stifled by the atmosphere of secrecy and suspicion bred by the Klan. The boycott, it is being discovered, does not increase business. In short, Oregon is finding out that the Klan as a social institution does not pay. The religious, political, business, and social discord that follow in its train are inimical to the material as well as to the spiritual interests of the community.

V

The story of the Klan in Oregon is most instructive as throwing light upon the significance of this order in American life. Here is a state composed of eighty-five percent native Americans. It has no race problem. It is predominantly Protestant in faith, the Catholics forming but eight percent of the population. It is not torn by industrial conflict. It is not threatened by radicalism in any form. It has progressive laws, an admirable educational system, less than two percent of illiteracy. Yet this typical American state has been completely overrun and, for a time at least, politically dominated by a secret oath-bound organization preaching religious bigotry and racial animosity and seeking primarily its own political aggrandizement. One asks how this is possible. The first outstanding fact is the impotence of public opinion where such a state of affairs is possible. There must be a singular lack of independent, critical public sentiment in a community that is such an easy victim of the Klan. One feels that the educational system of Oregon, in spite of one and one-half percent illiteracy, must be after all a very mechanical affair. Her sons and daughters, as in her sister states, pass with measured tread through public school, high school and university, assimilating the external mechanical symbols of culture, and yet these symbols remain mere symbols, traditional, educational and cultural stereotypes. These prospective citizens have not been schooled to the critical analysis of their intellectual heritage. So long as one is clever enough to clothe his propaganda in the familiar dress of these stereotypes he finds ready and uncritical acceptance.

A second observation suggested by the Oregon situation is the lack of the spirit of real tolerance in American society. When the Catholic Church established Newman Hall at the seat of Oregon's state university and sent an able priest, Rev. Edwin V. O'Hara, to look after the interests of Catholic students, thus taking a long step towards adjusting itself to the state system of education, the Klan was able, thanks to the ingrained intolerance of the community, to decry this as a deep and devilish Catholic scheme to overthrow Protestantism and set up the rule of the Pope. This is a most incredible and at the same time a most humiliating situation. It seems to indicate that the mass of Americans are still medieval in their thinking. There is food for thought in the fact that states like Oregon, Texas, Oklahoma, and Indiana, with low illiteracy, with admirable state systems of education culminating in great universities with thousands of students, are least immune to the propaganda of the Fundamentalists and the Ku Klux Klan. In spite of the millions spent on education it would appear that we do not really train our citizenship to *think* in matters of religion, politics, or economics. Religious tolerance requires, in a measure at least, reflection. It is more than the easy going, *laissez-faire* philosophy of the pioneer. It demands social imagination and the ability through sympathetic insight to enter into the inner life of our fellows. To the average Protestant the soul of the devout Roman Catholic is a sealed book.

CHAPTER III

THE SHADOW OF THE PAST

THE modern Ku Klux Klan is rooted in the past and for that reason can be properly judged only in the light of the historical perspective. The Klan is a highly complex social phenomenon and yet it is possible to distinguish two main sources from which it has sprung. Its name, methods, and paraphernalia were suggested by the Klan of Reconstruction days. Its ideals, on the other hand, or at least the objectives that have made it attractive to large groups of the American people, have been derived in the main from that great stream of social traditions and habits of thought which we may cover with the blanket term of Native Americanism. To the student of history it is perfectly obvious that for the antecedents of anti-Catholicism, anti-Semitism, and one hundred percent Americanism we must go, not to the Klan of Reconstruction days, but to such native American movements as the Know-Nothings of the middle of the last century

53

and the American Protective Association of the nineties. It is the object of this chapter to point out the connections between the modern Klan and the Klan of Reconstruction.

I

The old and the new Klans are similar in that both have been the objects of passionate hates and passionate loyalties. Sweet reasonableness has characterized neither their friends nor their foes. For example, a member of the United Daughters of the Confederacy asserts that when the tale of the South "is all told, and the history of her labors in war and peace has been recounted, no brighter chapter in all her history, no fairer page, will ever be read than that which tells of that illustrious and glorious organization called the Ku Klux Klan" (Mrs. S. E. F. Rose, *The Ku Klux Klan or the Invisible Empire*, p. 75). On the other hand, Senator John Sherman of Ohio, on the floor of the Senate Chamber, March 18, 1871, made use of the following language: "If any senator now, in looking over the record of crime of all ages, can tell me of an association, a conspiracy, or a band of men who combined in their acts and in their purposes more that is diabolical than this

Ku Klux Klan I should like to know where it is. They are secret, oath-bound; they murder, rob, plunder, whip, and scourge; and they commit these crimes, not upon the high and lofty, but upon the lowly, upon the poor, upon feeble men and women who are utterly defenseless.'' Truly an interesting statement coming from a representative of a state in which to-day the revived Klan probably numbers half a million. Similarly the modern Klan is inordinately praised as ''the most dauntless organization known to man'' and ministers of the Gospel of brotherly love and charity place the fiery cross side by side with the cross of Calvary in their churches. On the walls of a public building in a small Southern town the writer found scribbled, ''The K. K. K. are a bunch of yellow dogs; they have to hide their faces''; beneath this was written, ''King Solomon had nothing on the Pope and his harem at Rome,'' together with other things, unprintable in their language, indicating antagonisms hardly compatible with a healthful and happy community life. Wherever the Klan appears as a social issue we find unleashed some of the most unchristian and thoroughly despicable traits of human nature. The Klan loves a good hater.

Much light is thrown upon the modern Klan by

a knowledge of the atmosphere that surrounded its predecessor. It seems worth while, then, to examine for a moment the conditions that gave rise to the old Klan of the late sixties and early seventies. The atmosphere of the old Klan is admirably reproduced in the diary of a Southerner, Randolph Shotwell, written in a Northern prison during the early seventies, where he was confined because of alleged activities in the Ku Klux Klan in North Carolina.[1] Shotwell was a newspaper editor and was afterwards a member of the legislature of his state. The writer is indebted to Mr. Harris Dickson of Vicksburg, Mississippi, for access to the manuscript of this diary, which is not without historical value as being a first-hand account of these troublous times by a participant. This is the excuse for quoting it somewhat at length. The account, cast in dialogue form, is reproduced without criticism:

"*Ques.* Will you state the origin of the Klan?

"*Ans.* The Ku Klux Klan (using that familiar generic term for the several societies of which it was composed) was the legitimate offspring of

[1] The writer is indebted to Prof. J. G. de Roulhac Hamilton of the University of North Carolina for this statement with regard to Shotwell: "Undertaking in 1870 to check the excesses of the Ku Klux, which he had never joined, he was arrested for participation in a raid at which he was not present, and after a farce of a trial, preceded by very brutal treatment, he was sentenced to Albany for six years and was fined $5,000."

the Loyal Union League and the Freedmen's Bureau, and consequently owes its existence to radical legislation. [The Freedmen's Bureau was intended to mediate between ex-slave and former master and was therefore educative and social in purpose, though antagonistic to the prevailing Southern attitude. The Union League, a degenerate reproduction of a great original, was a corrupt and thoroughly unscrupulous political organization bent upon spoliation through the Negro vote.] The humiliations, the exactions, the persecutions and personal annoyances put upon the Southern people by the swarms of adventurers and sharpers which settled upon the land under the auspices of the Freedmen's Bureau and the Internal Revenue Department, can never be realized except by those who had the misfortune to experience them. Every town and village had its petty autocrat in uniform, whose mandates were *law* to the surrounding country and whose ill will was more to be feared than the presence of a hostile army. At this day it sounds laughable to tell of a martial hero, with drawn sword, chasing a half-witted countryman through the street of a peaceful town to cut a few rusty Confederate buttons off his jacket or sending a file of bayonets to arrest a respectable lady because her little girls had been seen playing in the back yard with something that looked like a Rebel flag. Yet such exploits were common in many parts of the South as late as 1867.

"From the first it was apparently the common object of all classes of Federal officials to excite an antagonism of races. No opportunity was lost to alienate the slave from his late master. The freedmen, uninfluenced by outsiders, would for the most part have continued to work and sing and dance on the old plantation content to receive a moderate allowance of the crop and sure to look to 'ole Massa' for advice and assistance in all troublous circumstances. But this would not do for the Bureau. The idle and vicious were lured from the farms by the issue of free rations, while the more industrious were kept in perpetual excitement by plausible reports that their former masters were plotting to put them back into slavery. The Bureau took cognizance of all disputes between Whites and Blacks and as no occasion was lost to browbeat the former for the diversion of the latter, Sambo was not slow in coming to the conclusion that the 'bottom rail was on top' sure enough.

"Any person acquainted with the excessive vanity and emotional nature of the Negro will not need to be told that his mind soon became unsettled and poisoned by such treatment. Nor will it appear strange that he was speedily duped into mental subjection to his new-found friends far more abject and binding than the physical restraint from which he had been so recently relieved. The immediate practical effect of the Bureau System was to collect the Negroes in towns, where they gave their attention to politics and privilege, while the farmers, for lack of hands, were obliged to reduce the number of acres under cultivation. To give an illustration: The city of Newbern, N. C., with a resident population of less than six thousand whites, had, in '66-'67, a floating population of near ten thousand Negroes, although only a few miles in the adjacent country farm servants could not be hired at any price. As might have been expected, crime and disorder were fearfully frequent. Being at the time associate Editor of *The Daily Journal of Commerce*, I had occasion to chronicle a dozen or more murders in less than half as many months. Burglary and highway robbery were the regular morning news items. Now in the sedate and law-abiding Old North State capital crimes have never been common and a murder makes a terrible noise, so that the new order of things created great alarm and indignation.

"At this juncture a far more threatening aspect was given to our domestic perplexities by the introduction of the Union League. Having long foreseen that Negro suffrage was inevitable, the wire-pullers of the Republican Party . . . began to scheme for the new political element (the Negro vote). There were already two secret societies in the state, the 'Red Strings' and the 'Heroes of America,' but the Negro had not been taken into them. . . . They (the Radicals) speedily enlisted the whole influence of the Government in favor of the League and in a few months there were not one hundred colored votes in the state, scarcely as many in the entire South, unbound by a secret oath to vote for the Radical candidates. Large numbers of timid and ignorant white men were likewise driven into this Radical Klan by dread of confiscation and loss of their civil privileges, it being asserted openly on the stump by League orators that the Government designed to take away the ballot from all who did not register on the Republican Rolls. I recollect hearing Judge Logan, one of the leaders of the League Party, publicly proclaim to an assemblage of excited Negroes that he *would rather enfranchise the dogs than the Rebels,* meaning the decent and intelligent portion of the community.

"The incompetency and corruption of the new judiciary was felt more than anything else, except the fearful multiplication of taxes, because the people of North Carolina have been accustomed to regard their courts with great pride and veneration. The new judges had been chosen, not for their ability or merit, but solely in regard to their service as party leaders. Several of them were notoriously incompetent: one is said habitually to have spelled January with a small 'g.' One or two of them were *and still are* charged with serious peculations.

"Throughout the South it was everywhere the same old story, the Negroes duped and corrupted by the Bureau, enticed into a secret, dark-lantern League, a Legislature controlled by carpet-baggers, a Governor with one hand in the treasury, a judiciary disgracing itself and making a mockery of the law! And everywhere the people groaning under intolerable taxes and sighing for peace. *We are now ready for the introduction of the Klan. The feeling had become almost universal that there should be some organization of good men for the suppression of crime and to counteract the pernicious teaching of the League.*"

Under the circumstances it was inevitable that such an organization should be secret and that it should draw its material from the members of the recent Confederacy.

II

It was Voltaire who said that *sa majesté le Hasard* has much to do with the development of the drama of history. Apparently it was accident that gave rise to the curious and awe-inspiring term "Ku Klux Klan." In May, 1866, a group of young men gathered in a law office of Pulaski, Tennessee, a small but cultured town near the Alabama line, and finding time hanging heavy on their hands after the stirring experiences of the war, decided to organize a club. The idea was enthusiastically received and various names were suggested, among them "Kukloi" the plural of the word *Kuklos*, the Greek for circle. "Ku Klux," a barbarization of *Kuklos*, was suggested by some one and at once adopted. To carry out the alliteration Klan was added, and hence the name Ku Klux Klan.

The newly organized Klan enjoyed great popularity during the summer and fall of 1866, and various "dens" were established in the country and towns in Tennessee, Alabama, Georgia, and even in remoter sections. By the spring of 1866, however, this organization had undergone a change by which it was transformed through the pressure of conditions described above into a secret society, the object of which was not pleasure but *social regulation*. Several things contributed to this transformation. In the first place the oath-bound secrecy, the atmosphere of mystery, the weird attire and ritual, when taken in connection with the prevailing disturbed condition of society, tended to convince outsiders and even the members of the Klan that it must have some more serious purpose than mere fun. More important, however, was the discovery that the secrecy and mystery of the weird costumes held altogether unforeseen possibilities for the control of the Negro population which, thanks to the policies of Reconstruction, was fast getting out from under the control of its old masters and under the leadership of carpet-baggers was being organized into the secret and powerful Union League to set up Negro rule.

This rôle of social regulators being thrust upon the Klan by force of social conditions, it became necessary to perfect its organization, to which end the Grand Cyclops of the Pulaski "den" called a convention in Nashville in the summer of 1867. At this meeting, attended by delegates from Tennessee, Alabama, Georgia, and other states the society was reorganized, a statement of principles adopted, officers appointed and assigned to different territories. The Klan was designated "the Invisible Empire." Its principles included "all that is chivalric in conduct, noble in sentiment, generous in manhood and patriotic in purpose." Its more specific objects were: (1) "To protect the weak, the innocent, the defenseless, from the indignities, wrongs, and outrages of the lawless, the violent, and the brutal; to relieve the injured and oppressed, to succor the suffering and unfortunate and especially the widows and orphans of Confederate soldiers. (2) To protect and defend the Constitution of the United States, and all laws passed in conformity thereto and to protect the states and the people thereof from all invasion from any source whatever. (3) To aid and assist in the execution of all constitutional laws and to protect the people from all unlawful seizure and from trial except by their peers in conformity with the laws of the land." The "Invisible Empire" was presided over by a Grand Wizard. The "realms," coterminous with the states, were ruled by Grand Dragons, the "dominions" or congressional districts by a Grand Titan, and each "den" by a Grand Cyclops. To these were added a Grand Monk, Grand Scribe, Grand Exchequer, Grand Turk, and a Grand Sentinel. Some of these titles it will be seen have been perpetuated in the modern Klan.

The Klan played a most important rôle in the overthrow of carpet-bag rule. A large number of Negroes, especially those living on the plantations, were rescued from the dominance of the Union League, though among the Negroes of the towns and cities the League still exercised considerable power. Burnings of cotton gins, petty thievery, and assaults upon women became rare. Labor was more dependable. The power of the scalawag and the carpet-bagger was broken, some of the most disreputable among them being driven from the country. But there were features of the Ku Klux Klan that went far to vitiate these good results. It was, in the first place, an organization that worked in secret and, secondly, it was forced, in spite of its lofty statements as to loyalty to constituted law, to accomplish its ends in extra-legal ways. These inherent weaknesses were not long in revealing themselves and finally brought the Klan itself into thorough disrepute among the best people of the South. As a Southern authority has said, they transformed "the Ku Klux Klan from a band of regulators, honestly trying

to preserve peace and order, into a body of des-
perate men who, in 1869, convulsed the country
and set at defiance the mandates of both state and
Federal governments.'' To be sure, the Grand
Dragon of the Realm of Tennessee issued a solemn warning, but all in vain. The Klan had
been instrumental in liberating forces of lawlessness which, thanks to its own inherent weaknesses,
the Klan was utterly unable to check. The better
men began to desert the order and in 1869 it was
formally disbanded by Grand Wizard Forrest, the
famous Confederate leader.

Though disbanded as a formal organization it
can hardly be said that the Klan ceased to exist.
The Grand Wizard's decree of dissolution never
reached all the various ''dens'' and they continued to exist, becoming more and more a law unto
themselves. As the better men left the order, the
criminal elements began to make use of it to further their ends until the Ku Klux Klan came to be
synonymous with every form of disguised lawlessness in a community that was fast verging upon
social chaos. The severe anti-Ku Klux laws
passed by the various carpet-bag governments
failed utterly. President Grant then intervened,
suspended the writ of habeas corpus, and placed
sections under martial law. It has been assumed

that "the vigorous supervision exercised by the Federal government in all parts of the South was instantly effective" (Oberholtzer, *History of the United States since the Civil War*, Vol. II, p. 390). So far as the immediate and superficial suppression of acts of violence was concerned this was perhaps true. But the real reason for the cessation of the Ku Klux "outrages" was that by this time the South had begun to regain home rule and was therefore in a position to accomplish by overt and more or less legal methods the ends it had been forced to seek in the days of oppression through the secret and extra-legal agency of the Klan.

III

In all the official utterances of the modern Klan a continuity of tradition is assumed to exist between it and the Klan of Reconstruction days. The letter-head scattered broadcast over the land from the "imperial aulic" at Atlanta bears at its top this legend, "The most sublime lineage in all history commemorating and perpetuating as it does the most dauntless organization known to man," and at its bottom, "In the name of our fathers—for country, our homes, and each other."

The cover pages of Klan literature bear the words, "We were here yesterday, we are here to-day, we will be here forever." The Kloran, containing the ritual of the Klan and written by Emperor Simmons, clearly presupposes the continuity of old Klan traditions, and the first degree is an extravagant eulogy of the old Klan. The original Klan organized by Simmons included four members of the old Klan and the Klan charter of 1915 may be looked upon as a sort of legal sanction for the appropriation of old Klan traditions, titles, costumes, and the like.

It was natural for some romantic Southerner to seek to revive the old Klan among a people who looked upon it as the defender of their homes and of their civilization in their struggle against cruel injustice and unparalleled oppression. It must be remembered that the South is the most romantically and uncritically sentimental of all sections of the country. It is unable to see a spot on the records of its heroes; an unvarnished narrative of the brute facts regarding the old Klan would appear to many Southerners little short of sacrilege. Finally, it must be remembered that the fearful years of Reconstruction served to ingrain deeply into the life of the South social habits that tend to condone extra-legal methods of attaining justice. Here, if anywhere, we must look for the explanation of the strange apathy of the masses of the South to the dangers of hooded and self-appointed regulators of the welfare of the community.

The question may very well be raised, however, as to why the modern revival of the old Klan should be so popular in the North. It seems by tradition and spirit to be a purely Southern institution. The social tradition in the North with regard to the Klan would seem indeed to be antagonistic. At the close of the war and for years afterwards the attitude of the masses of the North towards the Klan was doubtless in full sympathy with Senator John Sherman's denunciation of the Klan on the floor of the Senate, March 18th, 1871, quoted above. By a curious irony of fate the revived Ku Klux Klan, still ''secret,'' still ''oathbound,'' and still engaged in the business of whipping defenseless men and women, numbers several hundred thousand in Ohio, the state that gave John Sherman birth and which he represented in the United States Senate. What has brought about this transformation in the Northern attitude towards the Klan?

Many things have doubtless contributed to the modification of Northern sentiment in regard to

the Klan. First among these is the effect of the
mere flight of time. A half-century has elapsed
since Sherman pronounced his condemnation of
the Klan in the Senate. There has arisen a generation that "knows not Joseph" and that does
not understand the feelings of its fathers. There
is in the North generally (as opposed to the
South) a striking lack of continuity in social traditions. Communities like Boston and New England have undergone a complete transformation.
The Boston of Charles Sumner is now little more
than a pious memory. To the engulfing tide of
immigration which has swept away the old social
and racial traditions is to be added the disintegrating effect of industrialism. In the great manufacturing centers of New England and Pennsylvania about the only tie that unites men is the
impersonal bond of the daily wage. In the South,
on the other hand, there are large sections, as in
the Valley of Virginia, where family and culture
and social tradition still hold their own against
the dollar. In the industrial North, with its impersonal cash nexus, its welter of foreigners still
unassimilated, the Klan of Reconstruction days
was almost as unknown ten years ago as the
Knights Templars or the *Vehmgericht*.

There were, to be sure, forces at work in the

North paving the way for a sympathetic understanding of the old Klan, foremost among them
being the increased immigration of the Negro and
the consequent emergence of the "color line" in
those communities where the blacks were present
in large numbers. Ray Stannard Baker, in his interesting study, *Following the Color Line,* has
traced the gradual change of sentiment in the
North due to this increased pressure of racial
groups. But just a year or so before the organization of the modern Klan an event took place of
the very first importance in its influence upon
Northern sentiment toward the Klan, namely, the
production of David W. Griffith's great moving
picture, "The Birth of a Nation." It is simply
impossible to estimate the educative effect of this
film-masterpiece upon public sentiment. It is
probable that the great majority of adult Americans have at one time or another seen this film.
In the Boston theaters, where it was admitted
only after a bitter fight that served merely to ad-
vertise it, the picture was shown twice daily from
April to September, 1915, to a total of almost four
hundred thousand spectators. It broke the records in Boston and New York and in other large
cities. That the modern Klan recognized the advertising value of "The Birth of a Nation" seems

to be indicated in the proposal to make use of a
moving picture as part of the Klan propaganda
which "shows the hooded figures of the Knights
of the Ku Klux Klan riding to the rescue, and
portrays the final triumph of decent and orderly
government by real Americans over the alien influences now at work in our midst." It will doubtless always be a matter of debate whether the influence of "The Birth of a Nation" was predominantly good or bad. It did undoubtedly
make many aware for the first time of the wicked-
ness and injustice of the Reconstruction period.
The weakness of this picture does not lie so much
in its exaggeration of the evils of Negro domina-
tion in the South, an exaggeration permissible
perhaps in the interest of artistic effect, as
in the fact that it shows the Klan only in its best
aspects and before it had been made use of by
evil men for the perpetration of outrages even
worse than those it was designed to eliminate.

IV

Before the committee of Congress Emperor
Simmons emphatically disavowed, as we have seen,
any connection between the modern Klan and the
old Klan of Reconstruction days. This disavowal

is not borne out by the facts in regard to the activities of the modern Klan. The modern Klan reflects the methods and the spirit of the old Klan in many ways. Randolph Shotwell, in his account already quoted, states that the methods used by the old Klan were "at first of a somewhat ludicrous nature. In various parts of the country, where the Negroes had been most unruly, a huge terrific monster, giant, hobgoblin, or even Old Nick himself, stalked into the village on a moonlight night, and performed several supernatural feats, such as drinking two or three buckets of water or blowing an immense volume of flame from the nose, and after exhorting certain evildoers to beware of a second visit, suddenly departed amid such an infernal uproar that many old 'Aunties' will never believe that human agency had anything to do with it. Absurd and childish as it may seem, yet such a warning usually had stronger effect than all the penalties of the law in restraining the insolence and rowdyish propensities of the Negroes. Of course the more intelligent suspected the trick but as it implied a mystery or mysterious organization they were none the less awed."

In this rôle of social control through *intimidation* one of the most effective instruments, of

course, was the Klan costume. It is described as
a "long gown with loose flowing sleeves, with a
hood in which the apertures for the eyes, nose and
mouth are trimmed with some red material.
The hood has three horns, made of some common
cotton stuff, in shape something like candy bags,
stuffed and wrapped with red strings; the horns
stand out on the front and sides of the hood.
When a costume is worn by a person he is completely disguised by it. He does not speak in his
natural tone of voice and uses a mystical style of
language and is armed with a revolver, a knife,
and a stick." But these hooded regulators did
not depend upon their costume alone to subdue
the Negro. The costume was often equipped with
a leather bag, the use of which is indicated in the
following incident. "A night traveller called at
the Negro quarters somewhere in Attrakapas
(La.) and asked for water. After he had drunk
three blue buckets of good cistern water at which
the Negro was much astonished, he thanked the
colored man and told him he was very thirsty,
that he had travelled nearly a thousand miles in
twenty-four hours and that was the best drink of
water he had had since he was killed in the battle
of Shiloh. The Negro dropped the bucket, tumbled
over two chairs and a table, escaped through a

back window, and has not since been heard from. He was a radical Negro.'' Sometimes the ghostly riders carried skeleton hands concealed in their sleeves and insisted upon shaking hands with Negroes, with what effect can well be imagined. A hooded specter sometimes took off his head, supported by some artificial framework from the shoulders, and asked a horrified Negro to hold it until he could "fix his back-bone.'' What the effects of such childish pranks were upon the Negro just free from slavery can only be appreciated by one who has had first-hand knowledge of the extent to which the lives of the Negro peasantry of the far South are still ruled by superstition and fear.

Perhaps the most effective method used by the Klan to impress the community with a sense of its mysterious power was the nightly parade, a method still used with great effect by the revived Klan. The following description of the first parade of the Klan in Pulaski the fourth of July, 1867, is so closely paralleled by parades of the modern Klan that it may well be reproduced here. As a result of the printed notice, "The Klan will parade the streets to-night,'' an expectant crowd gathered from the town and surrounding country and lined the streets. "The members of the Klan in the country left their homes in the afternoon and travelled alone or in squads of two or three with their paraphernalia carefully concealed. . . . After nightfall they assembled at designated points. . . . Here they donned their robes and disguises and put covers of gaudy material on their horses. A skyrocket sent up from some point in the town was the signal to mount and move. The different companies met and passed each other in the public square in perfect silence; the discipline appeared to be admirable. Not a word was spoken. Necessary orders were given by means of whistles. In single file, in death-like stillness, with funereal slowness, they marched and counter-marched throughout the town. While the column was headed north on one street it was going south on another. By crossing in opposite directions the lines were kept up in almost un-broken continuity. The effect was to create the impression of vast numbers. This marching and counter-marching was kept up for about two hours and the Klan departed as noiselessly as they came. The public were more than ever mystified. . . . Perhaps the greatest illusion produced by it was in regard to the numbers participating in it. Reputable citizens were confident that the number was not less than three thousand. . . . The truth is that the number of the Ku Klux in the parade did not exceed four hundred.''

It will hardly be denied that the modern Klan has retained in its hood and gown, its silent parades and fiery torches, the very spirit and method of the old Klan. It still seeks to intimidate the community through the mysterious exhibit of its masked members. It still endeavors to control free and enlightened Americans through the fear of a vast and mysterious Invisible Empire that ''sees all and hears all.'' Now, to one familiar with the history of the old Klan this retention of its spirit and methods by the modern Klan is, to say the least, not very flattering to the citizenship of modern America. It implies that an intelligent and sovereign people can be controlled and manipulated as the ignorant Negro, fresh from the shackles of slavery, was controlled by the childish mummeries of the old Ku Klux Klan with its hideous masks, its skeleton hands, and its false heads. Such methods of procedure, it need only be suggested, are a gross insult to the intelligence and self-respect of a free people. They attribute to American citizens a childish susceptibility to the ghostly parades of masked mummers which one would expect to find to-day only among the inhabitants of a village of darkest Africa.

V

But even the Negroes of Reconstruction days
speedily outgrew this attempt to control them by
such childish means. The old Klan had to make
use of more strenuous methods. There is scarcely
a page of the thirteen volumes of the famous Ku
Klux investigations of 1871-2 that does not chronicle a whipping of Negro or white. The justification made by the old Klan was that murder and
rape and barn-burnings and riots were of frequent
occurrence and the control of the courts by the
corrupt Union League made it all but impossible
to bring the offenders to justice. Out of this condition developed the distinctive rôle of the old
Klan, namely, that of "a secret coöperative society of the nature of a vigilance committee or
patrol, designed to correct such civil abuses as did
not come within the purview of the law, or were
neglected by the officers of the law." The evidence which shows that the modern Klan, in its
practical operations in the communities where it
has been organized, has sought to perpetuate this
rôle of "a secret coöperative society of the nature of a vigilance committee or patrol" is simply overwhelming. Following the appearance of
the Klan the newspapers of Texas recorded some-

thing like eighty whippings in the state within a year. These were usually visited upon obscure and impotent members of the community who were moral and social outcasts. Effort at first was made to give these Klan activities publicity. A representative of the press was directed to be present at a certain time on some designated street corner after nightfall. He was then whisked away blindfolded to the place where the whipping was administered, and after having witnessed the whipping was returned by auto to the city, blindfolded. The places where these whippings occurred were located in some cases by means of the fragments of bloody shirts and broken suspenders of the victims.

The parallel between these whippings administered by the revived Klan and the whippings recorded in the thirteen volumes of the federal investigations of the old Klan in 1870-71 is most striking. Whipping was the favorite method of intimidating the Negro in Reconstruction days, the Klan seeking thereby to pry him loose from the control of carpet-bagger and radical Republican. These whippings are found in gruesome monotony in the records. There is this fundamental difference, however. The old Ku Klux who whipped Negroes, and occasionally whites,

were terribly in earnest because aroused by a
sense of unparalleled injustice and misrule. The
whippings by the revived Klan are prompted
by no such sense of intolerable wrong or indignation at political misrule. There is reason to
believe that in many cases these whippings are
a source of amusement and diversion provided
by the "strong-arm squad" of the local Klan.
The reports of the behavior of terrified Negroes
and outcast whites when snatched from their
homes under cover of night and whisked away
to some dark wood where they were thoroughly
thrashed must afford much amusement to these
secret and self-appointed guardians of public
morals as they listen to the story from the lips of
those assigned the task of maintaining "law and
order" in the community. It also flatters a per-
verted sense of moral righteousness and social importance. The worst phase of the whole story is
that these brutal and extra-legal ways of giving
expression to the moral sense of the community
often find commendation from such leaders of the
community as ministers. The deadly moral inertia
of communities where these outrages are passed
over with no attempt to vindicate the dignity of
the law gives us some insight into the mental atmosphere that makes the Klan possible.

The Klan authorities have, of course, uniformly denied any responsibility for these outrages. Owing to the secrecy with which the Klan seeks to cover all its acts, it is difficult to prove official responsibility. There is, however, evidence, both abundant and convincing, to show that in the case of local Klans these outrages were committed with local Klan sanction. What every self-respecting member of the Klan should bear in mind is that the organization has acquired a reputation which makes it possible to ascribe to it these outrages. If the Klan's secrecy prevents proof in each case of official responsibility, it likewise prevents the Klan from vindicating its good name. No militant secret order, except under abnormal social conditions such as Reconstruction in the South, can hope to enjoy the confidence and esteem of the best elements in the community. The mask is the millstone about the Klan's neck which, unless discarded, will sooner or later drown the Klan itself in the sea of hates and suspicions which it has created.

In striving to continue in our present-day society the "strong-arm" methods of the old Klan, its modern imitator has shown a singular lack of historical imagination. The avowed object of the old Klan was to overthrow by means of its secret

and oath-bound methods the nefarious carpet-bag
government which, the best citizens felt, had become a menace to the civilization of the South.
The modern Klan seeks to attain by the methods
of the old Klan ends which are diametrically opposed to the ends sought by the old Klan. The
modern Klan tells us on every occasion that it
stands for "law and order," for loyalty to the
Constitution, for the patriotic support of the existing government. The modern Klan can not see
that its mask and parades, its anonymous threatening letters, its childish attempts to intimidate
its enemies with the mysterious menace of a vast
Invisible Empire that "sees all and hears all" can
find no justification in a well-ordered society.
The modern Klan, judged by its methods, is a
glaring historic anachronism. The ends it claims
to seek and the means it uses to. attain those ends
are fundamentally incompatible. The ends are
"law and order," and yet the Klan makes use of
lawlessness and disorder to maintain law and order. The Klan stands for free speech and free
press, and yet the Klan in actual practice would
imprison the radical and forbid the Catholic to
defend his faith or to seek to win America to the
Catholic faith by a candid presentation of the
claims of his religion.

VI

Secrecy played a most important rôle in the old Klan and for reasons that are perfectly obvious. The Klan members were threatened with the loss of their freedom, their property, their homes, and perhaps their lives. Their only safety lay in an impenetrable oath-bound secrecy that would protect them from the corrupt and unscrupulous carpet-bag government which controlled the courts and the executors of the law. Secrecy was thus the very life of the old Ku Klux Klan. The modern Klan has undoubtedly been led, through its imitation of the old Klan, to give to the element of secrecy a place of exaggerated importance. Here again the Klan has shown a singular lack of historical imagination, for it has failed to see that in a free country governed by enlightened public opinion secrecy can only be tolerated when it is known to be in no wise inimical to public welfare. The element of secrecy appears, as is to be expected, in the multiplication of signs, gestures, grips, and passwords. In the oath of allegiance the candidate promises to "keep forever sacredly" the signs, words, grips, and "other matters of knowledge," and "never divulge the same nor even cause to be divulged to any person in the whole world unless I know positively that such a person is a member of this order in good and regular standing and not even then if it be for the best interests of the order.'' Here it will be observed that secrecy may be used against another member of the order if in the judgment of the individual it is best for the good of the order. The candidate swears that he ''will never yield to bribery, flattery, threats, passion, punishment, persecution, persuasion, or any enticements whatever coming from or offered by any person or persons, male or female, for the purpose of obtaining from me a secret or secret information of the . . . I will die rather than divulge the same, so help me God. Amen.'' Again in section four we read, ''I swear that I will keep secure to myself a secret of a Klansman when same is committed to me in the sacred bond of Klansmanship, the crime of violating this solemn oath, treason against the United States of America, rape, and malicious murder alone excepted.'' It is, of course, a dubious ethical procedure to put the violation of the oath of a fraternal order on a par with such grave crimes as murder, rape, and treason.

For the purposes for which Emperor Simmons repeatedly tells us the Klan was founded, namely, fraternity, patriotism, and brotherhood, this oath of strenuous secrecy seems entirely unnecessary. Were men engaged in an arduous struggle for the maintenance of their civilization, as the men of Reconstruction days conceived they were engaged, such an oath might be justifiable, but in peaceable, orderly, present-day America such an oath is an egregious anachronism. Furthermore, there is reason to suspect that this oath has exercised a baneful influence upon the practical workings of the Klan. It has taught Klansmen to trust to secrecy and mystery and even intimidation to secure their ends rather than to enlightened and frank expression of opinion. It lends justification to concealment within the Klan itself so that the sentiment of the Klan as a whole can not be brought to bear upon the acts of groups or individuals operating behind the mask and robe. Finally, this oath has undoubtedly exercised a subtle suggestive influence upon Klansmen themselves. It has served to convince Klansmen that theirs is a militant order with stern duties involving danger and discomfort. For if the Klansman's life is not strenuous, why this insistence upon keeping everything connected with the Klan a deep secret? The psychological effect of this upon local Klans has undoubtedly been to encourage "strong-arm methods" in their attempts to

"clean up" the community. The bitter opposition
these secret methods have aroused among Klan
opponents has simply confirmed many Klansmen
in their belief in the heroic knight-errantry of
their mission.

VII

A questionnaire sent out by the writer to determine the reasons for joining the Klan revealed
an interesting fact. Purity of womanhood as a
Klan ideal is mentioned only by correspondents
from the South. It does not occur among the
Klan objectives mentioned by correspondents
from the North and West. This fact has attracted the attention of a student of the Klan who
sees in it evidence of the abnormal sensitiveness
of Southern society to all matters of sex, due primarily, he thinks, to the racial situation in that
section (Frank Tannenbaum, "The Ku Klux
Klan," *The Century*, 1923, pp. 873ff.). Mr. Tannenbaum finds evidence here for the existence of
what he calls a "defense mechanism which some
Southerners have constructed against loose moral
standards" in their relations with colored women.
"The idealization of the white women in the South
is thus partly the unconscious self-protection on

the part of the white men from their own bad
habits, notions, beliefs, attitudes and practices.''
This appeal to Freudianism for an explanation of
the Southerner's mental attitude towards womanhood is of doubtful value. It is true that the racial situation of the South does condition the idea
of Southern womanhood but not in any mysterious
Freudian sense. The white woman is the citadel
of the white race's purity in the South, as in all
other countries where whites and blacks are
thrown together. When white women mate freely
with black men the color line, and with it racial
integrity, will soon disappear. The recognition
of this tends naturally to throw around the Southern white woman something of a sacrosanct atmosphere not to be found in the other sections of
the country where the race question is not so
acute.

It may be seriously doubted, however, whether
the racial situation has had as much to do with the
emphasis upon purity of womanhood by the Klan
in the South as the traditions inherited from the
Klan of the Reconstruction. This is indicated by
the following extracts from the diary of Randolph
Shotwell previously quoted, who states that ''war
has left so many thousands of widows and defenseless females on isolated plantations'' that it

became one of the primary duties of the old Klan
"to shield our women and children from the insolence, rapacity, and brutal passions of vile desperadoes, white and black. So well is this under-
stood in the South that you will find but few of
our noble ladies to-day who do not sympathize
warmly with the convicted Ku Klux in this prison.
They do not approve of every act, particularly the
more violent ones, committed by, or at least attributed to, the Klan. But they know that its general
aims were good, and feel indebted to it for a certain degree of safety which they could not have
had without it." This tradition still persists in
the South. Reference has already been made to
an extravagant glorification of the old Klan by
a Southern woman, Mrs. S. E. F. Rose, in her book
The Ku Klux Klan, "unanimously endorsed by
the United Daughters of the Confederacy in convention assembled."

The continuity of the old and new Klans is further evinced by the fact that the old Ku Klux Klan
traditions have never died out, especially in the
South. We have seen that owing to the chaotic
conditions in the South about 1868 the local
"dens," either because they did not get the decree
dissolving the order or because they did not wish
to see it dissolved, continued to enjoy a casual

and independent local existence of their own. The Klan tradition persisted and only needed conditions of social strain to give it new life. We have had in various sections of the South and elsewhere since Reconstruction days the constant recurrence of disturbances in which "white-caps" or "night-riders" have made use of Klan methods. In north Georgia, for example, in the late eighties and early nineties there arose a powerful organization, composed originally of moonshiners of the mountains, but gradually developing into a semi-political secret order, which used the disguise and even the name of the Ku Klux Klan. They terrorized the country until wiped out by the federal authorities.

Whenever and wherever there are conditions of social unrest in the less settled sections of this country we find a marked tendency to fall back upon the extra-legal methods of securing justice of which the old Klan is perhaps the most striking example in our national history. Conditions of social strain were created by the great war, the effects of which emerged in the post-war period when the modern Klan started upon its remarkable growth. The year 1920, which witnessed the emotional upheaval registered in the vigorous repudiation of Wilson and his League of Nations, was also the year in which the Klan entered upon its nation-wide expansion. The time was ripe for a revival of the old Klan, the traditions of which had never ceased to exist in more or less sporadic form, especially in the South.

The outstanding characteristic of the old Klan in its degenerate stage, the trait likewise characteristic of the sporadic revivals of Klan traditions since Reconstruction and emerging again in the modern Klan, is the lawless self-sufficiency of the local Klan or organization. Each "den" of the old disbanded Klan became a law unto itself. Hence the "outrages" of the old Klan, hence the menace of the sporadic revivals of the Klan traditions since Reconstruction, and hence the fundamental weakness of the modern Klan. The story of the Mer Rouge tragedy in northern Louisiana, which finds parallels in many other sections where the local Klan has taken matters into its own hands, indicates that the modern Klan is structurally weak in that it does not have, and from the nature of its secret methods can not have, any effective control of local Klans by the central authorities. The Klan is thus essentially and inherently a lawless organization.

VIII

The history of the old Klan finds another parallel in that of the modern Klan; both have been opposed by the most intelligent members of the community. It is a mistake to suppose that the old Klan enjoyed the unanimous sanction of all members of the Southern communities suffering from Negro rule in Reconstruction days. Robert W. Shand, a prominent lawyer of Unionville, South Carolina, writing under the pseudonym "Brutus" in the *Weekly Union Times* for July 17th, 1871, states: "There are some erroneous opinions entertained as to the feelings of the people of Upper South Carolina towards the Ku Klux. They are not a band of cut-throats and desperadoes, as some suppose; nor, on the other hand, are they universally approved by the white people here. They are men of firmness and nerve who strike because they believe it is necessary for the protection of their life, property and liberty; they strike at night because circumstances render it imperative. But very many citizens disapprove and condemn the acts of violence committed by the Klan. We feel the oppression of the present state government but we would not have it overturned by violence. . . . We are no apologists for the Ku Klux. Nothing here written is an apology. The reader who so construes this letter finds *excuse* sufficient in what we have enumerated simply as *causes*. We can not excuse the self-constituted avengers of white men's wrongs. Crime begets crime but does not excuse it. To kill a man is murder. To be prosecutor, judge, jury, and sheriff is a fearful sin—a sin legally and morally and a sin in His eyes to whom belongeth vengeance. We may have no justice but it is better to suffer and wait. A bad government is better than no government at all. Injustice is better than anarchy." In an editorial comment on this letter the *Weekly Union Times* says, "Nine out of every ten who read Brutus' letter will cordially endorse, its sentiments and truthfulness."

Just as in the case of the old Klan, there is in every community where the modern Klan is active a minority who oppose it. An analysis of this minority is most suggestive. In general, those of independent mind are opposed to the Klan. There is little doubt that ex-Senator Le-Roy Percy of Greenville, Mississippi, is correct when he states, "The thinking element of the community is against the Klan." The following statement from a prominent clergyman of Georgia is typical of the attitude of the independent-minded ministers: "The Klan is a useless organization and will serve no particular purpose. By the best citizens it seems to be looked upon with disfavor and some have been prompt and vehement in denying that they have ever belonged to it." In the city of Atlanta the Klan is looked upon with disfavor by the liberal-minded and progressive clergy and they seem to have the support of their churches. It is unfortunate that they have not seen fit to voice their condemnation. The Klan is opposed by eighty-five percent of the newspapers and for obvious reasons. The newspaper exists to provide publicity, and its usefulness, even its very existence, is menaced by the secret methods of the Klan. The bankers are generally opposed to the Klan. Where bankers have made the mistake of identifying themselves with the Klan economic pressure from Catholics and Jews has often forced them to resign from the Klan. Members of the bar, especially judges, are generally opposed to the Klan for they recognize in its extra-legal methods of attaining justice a distinct danger to the dignity and efficiency of the law. Many members of these various groups, who at first identified themselves with the Klan and afterwards resigned, are to be found in every community. Not so much the number as the character of these men constitutes their importance. Their attitude provides a most convincing argument against the Klan.

CHAPTER IV

CONCERNING KLAN PSYCHOLOGY

THE student of the Klan finds some curious paradoxes in the solution of which he is apt to go amiss unless he takes into consideration the mental processes of the Americans of the old native stock who compose the rank and file of the Klan membership. To read the newspaper accounts of alleged Klan outrages, such as the Mer Rouge murders, the whippings of Texas, the secret proscription of American citizens, the un-Christian arraignment of Catholics and Jews by Klan preachers, the childish mummeries of hood and gown, the spectacular initiations in the light of blazing torches, and the solemn nightly parades in the presence of gaping thousands of mystery-loving Americans—to read of these and to listen to the arraignments of the Klan by its enemies inclines one to feel that the members of this order are a curious combination of ferocious cruelty, cowardly vindictiveness, superstitious ignorance, and religious bigotry. On the other hand, when one converses with the members of the Klan, as the writer has done, he finds them to be conventional Americans, thoroughly human, kind fathers and husbands, hospitable to the stranger, devout in their worship of God, loyal to state and nation, and including in many instances the best citizens of the community. What is the explanation of the apparent contradiction? The explanation, in so far as there is any explanation of the hodgepodge of hopes and fears, of lofty ideals and brutish passions which we call human nature, is to be found in the psychology of that element in our population that is attracted by the Klan.

I

By a process of elimination it is possible to demarkate with a fair degree of accuracy the general class from which the Klan draws its members. The twenty millions of Catholics, the twelve millions of Negroes, the two millions and more of Jews, and the twenty millions of foreign-born are automatically excluded from membership by the Klan constitution. Organized labor is not in sympathy with the Klan. The American Federation of Labor at its convention in Cincinnati, June 12-24, 1922, "unanimously adopted" the following report: "Your committee is of the opinion that the American Federation of Labor should not assume to endorse or condemn any organization, fraternity, or association of American citizens unless the purpose of such organization is to organize for the purpose of interfering with the rights, opportunities and liberties of wage earners. Your committee is firmly of the opinion that the administration of the law is vested solely and entirely in the duly elected and appointed officers of the law, and that those who as members of any secret organization assume to usurp the functions properly belonging to legal authorities, invite mob-rule and create in men's minds a disrespect for and a disregard of duly constituted authority. Your committee is also of the opinion that it is not conducive to government by law and the maintenance of peaceful and safe conditions in the community to have members of any organization parade the streets so disguised that their identity can not be discovered when such disguises are adopted for the purpose of inspiring the thought or belief that the disguised individuals represent an invisible government." The Klan, as might be expected from its policy of opportunism, has on occasion, as in Kansas when it seemed to further Klan interests, championed the cause of labor. But there is little in common between Klan doctrines and those of organized labor. The average Klansman is far more in sympathy with capital than with labor. There are sporadic instances of workers, generally skilled workers, identifying themselves with the Klan, but the Klan has made no great inroad upon labor, skilled or unskilled.

Mr. James R. Howard, president of the American Farm Bureau Federation, "an organization of more than a million farmers," states: "My work has taken me into every section of the country and given me exceedingly broad contacts with representatives of all industrial and commercial organizations as well as agricultural. I have yet to come in contact with the first trace of Ku Klux Klanism and have never heard mention or reference to it except through the press." This rather remarkable statement from one enjoying unrivalled opportunities for observation among the farming population would seem to indicate that the Klan has no great hold upon the farmer. There are undoubtedly many farmers who are members of the Klan. Local Klans have been organized in the agricultural communities in various Southern states and presumably in the North and West. There is every reason to believe, however, that this great reservoir of native Americanism, which has very real affiliations with the Klan, has never been exploited. The explanation lies not in antagonism to the Klan, but rather in the natural difficulties of maintaining effective Klan organization in the country. The Klan is essentially a village and small-town organization. Neither the great city with its hodgepodge of races and groups nor the country with its isolation lends itself to effective Klan organization.

It would seem, then, that the Klan draws its members chiefly from the descendants of the old American stock living in the villages and small towns of those sections of the country where this old stock has been least disturbed by immigration, on the one hand, and the disruptive effect of industrialism, on the other. As is to be expected, therefore, we find the Klan fairly strong in the South, where the percentage of the old American stock is highest and where it has been left in undisturbed possession of its traditions, in parts of the Middle West, and in states like Oregon.

By far the majority of the native whites of the South are the descendants of the Scotch-Irish who came to America in two great streams during the eighteenth century, one stream striking in through New Jersey and Pennsylvania, crossing

the Alleghenies and following down the Ohio, the
other coming in through the Carolinas and the
Valley of Virginia and providing the pioneers
who opened up the South and Southwest. This
poor white Scotch-Irish stock in the South lived
a more or less submerged existence during the
slavery régime. Towards the close of the last
century they suddenly awoke to a sense of their
power. Under the leadership of such politicians
as Tilman of South Carolina, Vardaman of Mississippi, Jeff Davis of Arkansas, and Tom Watson of Georgia they made themselves the political masters of the South as they had already
dominated that section religiously and morally.

To understand the spread of the Klan in the
South one must understand the mental attitudes
of this old Scotch-Irish stock in Southern society.
They are intensely Protestant. Originally Pres-
byterians, they are now for the most part members of the Baptist and Methodist communions.
The Baptists, the most numerous denomination in
the South, with a membership of three and one half
millions, are apparently the religious mainstay of
the Klan. It is probable that the majority of
the Baptist ministers in the small towns and countryside are either secretly or openly sympathetic
with the Klan. The Klud, or official chaplain of

the Klan, Rev. Caleb Ridley, was a member of the Baptist Association of Atlanta. From their Presbyterian ancestry these Scotch-Irish have inherited the most intense and unreasoning antipathy to the Roman Catholic Church. This antipathy often makes itself felt in communities where the Catholics are in a hopeless minority, as in Georgia where they number at most only a few thousand.

As in few other sections of the country, the old native American stock of the South is often the victim of its own noble but uncritical and passionate loyalties. The Southern voter is prone to accept uncritically all forms of half-baked radicalism in politics bearing the label of the orthodox Democratic party, such as the Sub-Treasury scheme, Free Silver, and Populism. A beautiful but unreasoning loyalty to orthodox Protestantism induces Southern Protestants to swallow with the same uncritical avidity the crude ejaculations of Mr. Bryan and the Fundamentalists against Evolution and Modernism in religion. It is this mental background with its provincial fear of all things foreign and its uncritical but loyal Americanism which we must presuppose in order to understand the sympathetic reception of the following utterance of Emperor Simmons in an address to the Junior Order of United Mechanics in Atlanta,

April 30th, 1923: "My friends, your government can be changed between the rising and the setting of one sun. This great nation with all it provides can be snatched away from you in the space of one day. . . . When the hordes of aliens walk to the ballot box and their votes outnumber yours, then that alien horde has got you by the throat. . . . Americans will awake from their slumber and rush out to battle and there will be such stir as the world has never seen the like. The soil of America will run with the blood of its people."

It would be a gross injustice to the South to imagine, however, that the prejudices and fears appealed to by Klan leaders are entertained by all members of the community. The *intelligentsia* of the South, as of other sections, are opposed to the Klan, though they are, of course, a very small minority. There are men of independent mind in every Southern state who have spoken out in no uncertain terms against the Klan, such as ex-Senator LeRoy Percy of Greenville, Mississippi, Mr. Melville Foster of the *Houston Chronicle*, Rev. Ashby Jones, the eloquent Baptist minister of Atlanta. In every hamlet there are earnest and thoughtful men and women who are opposed to the Klan. Almost without exception the leaders in the various professions and in business are not in sympathy with the Klan. The strength of the Klan lies in that large, well-meaning but more or less ignorant and unthinking middle class, whose inflexible loyalty has preserved with uncritical fidelity the traditions of the original American stock. This class is perhaps more in evidence in the South than in any other section of the country. The Klan leaders have been able to play upon their prejudices and unreasoned loyalties with success exactly for the same reasons that these loyalties have been manipulated by political spellbinders such as Vardaman, Tom Watson, and Bryan. The most dangerous weakness in a democracy is the uninformed and unthinking average man.

II

The Klan, however, appeals to other sections as well as to the South. What are the psychological factors, common to the mind of America as a whole, which have paved the way for the national expansion of the Klan? The original Klan, as we have seen, was organized by a group of young men in the little village of Pulaski, Tennessee, who had recently returned from the war and found time hanging heavy on their hands.

This organization with its mysterious signs, its queer name, its fantastic costume, and its ritual offered some relief from the deadly monotony of small town life. The same psychological need for escape from the drabness of village and small town life plays no small part in the appeal of the modern Klan to the average American. Sinclair Lewis has portrayed for us in *Main Street* the monotony of existence in the small town of the Middle West. In his later story, *Babbitt,* he sketched with the pen of a master the business man of native American stock caught in the grip of traditional, unreflective, and uninspiring one-hundred-dred-percent Americanism. To this large group the appeal of the Klan is almost irresistible. It falls in entirely with their traditional Americanism while offering at the same time through its mystery a means of escape from the wearisome monotony of their daily round. Its cheap moral idealism fills a need not met by business or social and civic life.

The dreariness of small-town life in the Middle West analyzed so skilfully by Sinclair Lewis exists, perhaps, in even greater intensity, in that vast area stretching from the straggling foothills of the Blue Ridge Mountains across central and southern Georgia, Alabama, Mississippi, northern

Louisiana, Texas, Arkansas, and Oklahoma. There are parts of this region, such as northern Louisiana, eastern Texas, Arkansas, and Oklahoma, which for drabness and deadly monotony at the higher spiritual and intellectual levels are hardly to be paralleled anywhere else in America. The poverty of soul is brought out in all the more ghastly distinctness by the hectic activity in the accumulation of wealth through the exploitation of oil fields or otherwise. Here the followers of Mr. Bryan manifest their passionate devotion to science by prying loose from their chairs professors in the state universities who teach evolution. Here the Fundamentalists, the defenders of evangelical orthodoxy, seek to win the eternal commendation of God by unfrocking the minister who impeaches Moses's claim to the authorship of the Pentateuch. Here the dweller in the small town and countryside follows the monotonous and unimaginative round of his nights and days untouched by the beauty and mystery of life. At the higher levels of religion and morals he is tyrannized over by the Puritanical precepts of an orthodox Protestantism which places a premium upon the mental servility of "simple" faith, taboos forms of worldly amusements without troubling to find a substitute, and dooms its devotees to a

life spent in the midst of spiritual and moral il-
lusions. A keen critic of American life has remarked that conventional Protestantism, still by
far the most powerful factor in the higher life of
Americans, "hides the edges of the sea of life
with a board-walk of ethical concepts and sits
thereon, hoping that no one will hear the thunder
of the surf of human passions on the rocks below."

It was in this great southwestern area dominated
by orthodox Protestantism that the Klan reached
its first peak of success. To understand its remarkable spread we must enter sympathetically
into the life of the people. We must realize the
appeal of its mystery to imaginations starved by
a prosaic and unpoetic environment. We must
try to feel as they feel the dramatic interest
aroused by the weird costumes, the spectacular
initiations beneath the glare of fiery torches, the
nightly parades through quiet hamlets where men
and women gather from far and near to gaze on
this strange apparition. The mayor of a small
Texas town, describing to the writer the attitude
of the thousands gathered to witness a Klan parade, stated that as the mysterious cavalcade filed
silently down the street, hooded and sheeted, bearing a fiery cross at its head, one could almost hear

the breathing of the crowd. Here was something that broke the deadly monotony of their days, that symbolized the uncharted realm of an Invisible Empire, that fascinated by its appeal to the supernal. The effect was much like that produced upon the villagers of South Germany or Italy when on certain religious occasions the image of a patron saint is borne through the streets to the solemn chant of monks and the odor of swinging censers. The Klan has learned, as its inveterate enemy, the Roman Catholic Church, learned long ago, the power of the appeal to the spectacular and the mysterious.

The Klan makes a powerful appeal to the petty impotence of the small-town mind. A close observer of the Klan from Texas makes the following suggestive remark: "There is a great 'inferiority complex' on the part of the Klan membership—due in part to lack of education—Dallas and Fort Worth (where the Klan is especially strong) being largely populated by men and women reared in obscure towns and country places where public schools are short-termed and scarce." Here we have a curious side-light upon the psychology of the average man of native American stock who fills the ranks of the Klan. He is tossed about in the hurly-burly of our in-

dustrial and so-called democratic society. Under
the stress and strain of social competition he is
made to realize his essential mediocrity. Yet according to traditional democratic doctrine he is
born free and the equal of his fellow who is outdis-
tancing him in the race. Here is a large and
powerful organization offering to solace his sense
of defeat by dubbing him a knight of the Invisible Empire for the small sum of ten dollars.
Surely knighthood was never offered at such a
bargain! He joins. He becomes the chosen con-
servator of American ideals, the keeper of the
morals of the community. He receives the label
of approved "one hundred percent Americanism." The Klan slogan printed on the outside
of its literature is "an urgent call for men." This
flatters the pride of the man suffering from the
sense of mediocrity and defeat. It stimulates his
latent idealism. It offers fantastic possibilities
for his dwarfed and starved personality. Membership in a vast mysterious empire that "sees
all and hears all" means a sort of mystic glorification of his petty self. It identifies his own weak
incompetent will with the omnipotent and universal will of a great organization. The appeal
is irresistible. There are of course others who

see in this secret and powerful organization opportunities for gratifying individual ambition. Strong but unscrupulous men have availed themselves of the Klan to attain their selfish ends. On the whole, however, the high-minded and independent members of the community do not identify themselves with the Klan. It is a refuge for mediocre men, if not for weaklings, and for obvious reasons.

III

One finds on every page of Klan literature an insistent, imperative, and even intolerant demand for like-mindedness. It is, of course, the beliefs and traditions of the old native American stock that are to provide the basis for this like-mindedness. The Catholic is free to entertain his own ideas in religion but he must feel, think, and act in terms of pure and unadulterated Americanism. The foreign-born member of the community is tolerated only on the presupposition that he learns the American tongue, adopts the American dress and conventionalities, in a word assimilates as quickly and thoroughly as possible the traditions of the old American stock. The eternal quarrel of the Klan with the Jew and the Negro is that mental and physical differences seem to have conspired to place them in groups entirely to themselves so that it becomes to all intents and purposes impossible for them to attain with anything like completeness this like-mindedness synonymous with one hundred percent Americanism. The Negro is granted a place in American society only upon his willingness to accept a subordinate position, for one hundred percent Americanism means white supremacy. The Jew is tolerated largely because native Americanism can not help itself. The Jew is disliked because of the amazing tenacity with which he resists absolute Americanization, a dislike that is not unmingled with fear; the Negro is disliked because he is considered essentially an alien and unassimilable element in society.

Back of the Klan's insistence upon like-mindedness there is, to be sure, a measure of democratic common sense. If there is to be any sort of effective and intelligent social coöperation a measure of agreement upon fundamentals is necessary. Within the social order, to be sure, there will always be group and class differences. These differences may be made a most valuable means of cultivating a vigorous and enlightened citizenship.

It is a peculiarity of human thinking that truth is far more apt to emerge where we discuss our differences than where we emphasize our agreements. It is only when these differences cut so deeply that they threaten the integrity of the social tissue that they become dangerous. To play the game of citizenship successfully there must be a punctilious regard for the "rules of the game" that all contestants have agreed to observe. The Klan belongs to the crop of patriotic organizations that sprang up during and after the war and have for their general object the preservation of that measure of like-mindedness which was felt to be, absolutely necessary not only for the prosecution of the immediate task of winning the war but also for coping successfully with the welter of problems created by the war. To this extent the Klan undoubtedly represents the natural reaction of conservative Americans against the perils of revolutionary and un-American ideas. It is a militant attempt to secure team-work in national life.

Back of the Klan's crude insistence upon like-mindedness, however, there is much shallow and superficial thinking. To the average Klansman what appears on the surface of things to be alike is alike, what appears unlike is unlike. The acci-

dent of a black skin is made an excuse for de-
barring from the charmed circles of one hundred
percent Americanism a man who may be, in spite
of his Negro blood, intensely, intelligently, and
patriotically American. On the other hand, a man
with the external earmarks of the old American
stock is accepted uncritically as a one hundred
percent American. All the Klan asks is a superficial conformity. For the average Klansman, apparently, one hundred percent Americanism is
often identified with the crude and unreasoned
emotional enthusiasms that are excited by external
symbols such as the flag, the soldier's uniform, or
the words of the Declaration of Independence.
There is reason to believe that, just as the primi-
tive savage creates for himself a grotesque image
of his enemy, sticks his dagger into it, and ima-
gines that he has thereby done his enemy to death,
so many members of the Klan create a mental
image of the Pope that in actual reality bears little or no resemblance to that reverend gentleman,
and then proceed to belabor this mental fiction
with fierce un-Christian invectives. A child whipping its contumacious dolly is hardly more irrational.

IV

The mental attitudes emphasized by the Klan
under the labels of one hundred percent Americanism, anti-Catholicism, and the like, consist for
the most part of a set of external and factitious
mental symbols that often have little or no cor-
respondence with reality. The Klansman, like the
mass of average Americans, lives and moves in a
world of mental stereotypes.[1]   In his famous
allegory of the cave Plato says: "Behold! human
beings living in a sort of underground den, which
has a mouth open towards the light and reaching
all across the den; they have been here from their
childhood, and have their legs and necks chained
so that they can not move, and can only see before them; for the chains are arranged in such
manner as to prevent them from turning around
their heads.   At a distance above and behind them
the light of a fire is blazing, and between the fire
and the prisoners there is a raised way; and you
will see if you look a low wall built along the way,
like the screen which marionette players have before them, over which they show the puppets."
As men and animals walk along the wall their
shadows are projected by the fire upon the back

[1] See Walter Lippmann's *Public Opinion*.

wall of the cave so that the men chained in the cave "see only their own shadows or the shadows of one another which the fire throws upon the opposite wall of the cave." This famous figure of the old Greek sage describes in poetic form the mental conditions under which the majority of men live. It is a shadow world composed of mental pictures of external reality. If these pictures are false their world is unreal; if true their world is real.

Plato's famous allegory of the cave falls short in one very important particular. The mental pictures by which we represent the external world are not pictures that are projected mechanically upon the moving-picture screen of our souls. They are in reality outgrowths of experience, artifacts that are created by social contacts in family, church, club, party, class, nation, race. Darwin or the Pope exist and take on practical significance mainly as sectarian artifacts. That is to say, the mental pictures that stand for the real personal head of the Church of Rome vary in pronounced fashion according as the Pope is imagined by a Baptist Klansman of Georgia, a Unitarian of Back Bay, Boston, or an Irish Catholic of Cork. Similarly, the Darwin damned by Georgia Baptist or admired by Boston Unitarian is to all intents and purposes in each case an artifact, that is to say, a more or less artificial mental symbol which has slowly taken shape under the pressure of family, church, school, and community so that each particular mental picture of Darwin, the product of different local conditions, stands in the thought and life of each of these individuals for the actual historic Darwin.

Men and women act upon the assumption that these mental symbols or artifacts by which they picture to themselves the world actually correspond with the utmost fidelity to reality. That is to say, they identify their ideas of men and things with the absolute truth as to men and things. There are tens of thousands of devout Klansmen of the South and Middle West who have built up, under the tutelage of orthodox pastors and such intellectual leaders as Mr. Bryan, certain mental pictures with regard to the Pope or evolution. They act upon the assumption that these mental pictures actually correspond to the ultimate facts. They conclude that the Roman Catholic Church is subversive of all true Americanism and hostile to the national educational ideal. Acting upon this assumption, they bring pressure to bear upon their legislatures, as in Oregon, to eliminate the Catholic parochial schools. These mental pictures have all the practical implications in conduct, therefore, of actual reality. The seriousness with which men take their mental pictures, the bewildering fashion in which these mental pictures vary from group to group and the appalling difficulty we meet when we try to reconcile all these various mental pictures or seek to bring them into some sort of harmony with the actual facts, all combine to give us some insight into the exasperating difficulties that beset the problem of rational social control. The problem of the Klan is the problem of stubborn, uncritical mental stereotypes.

Obviously the world of immediate practical importance for the student of society is this world of mental artifacts, the pictured world that men carry around in their heads. This pictured world tends to take the place of the real world for all of us, Catholic and Protestant, scientist and rustic, Klansman and anti-Klansman. We adjust our conduct to fixed mental pictures of men and things or "mental stereotypes," as Walter Lippmann calls them in his suggestive book, *Public Opinion*. Men fight and die for their fictive mental worlds. In the early days of the Christian Church longshoremen in the city of Alexandria, Egypt, gave each other bloody noses over the question as to whether Jesus, the second person of the Trinity, was of the *same* or *like* substance with the Father, the first person of the Trinity. Men have lost their reason brooding over the mental picture of a personal devil or the pangs of eternal torment in hell fire. Thousands of the members of the Klan have stereotyped conceptions of all foreigners as Bolshevists, of labor unions as socialistic, of men with black skins as essentially inferior to men with white skins, of the Pope as the anti-Christ of the book of Revelation, and of every Catholic as an actual or potential traitor to his country. The vast majority of these good people have never taken the trouble to criticize these mental stereotypes. They took them over from their heritage of conventional American traditions much as the chameleon takes on the color of the green leaf upon which it rests. Any one who dared suggest to the average Klansman that his mental stereotypes as to the Pope, the Constitution, the Jew, or white supremacy were merely ways of looking at things with no special claim to trustworthiness would be considered a very uncomfortable individual or else a candidate for the lunatic asylum.

Much might be said in defense of stereotypes as part of our mental furniture. They are useful in that they are economical. Each stereotype may

be looked upon as coin current, struck out of the
crude ore of social experience. We use these
stereotypes because they spare us the trouble of
going through all the experience of the past that
is crystallized and condensed into a mental stereotype. Think of all the mental wear and tear the
average man is saved by the mental stereotypes
struck out for him in radical, socialist, atheist,
Bolshevist, higher criticism, evolution, white supremacy, democracy, the divinity of Jesus, purity of womanhood, free speech, or one hundred
percent Americanism. These stereotypes are pas-
sively assimilated by the child in the home, the
church, the school, the community. They literally
close down upon the child's budding mental life
and shape it as the molds shape the potter's clay.
These stereotypes economize time and mental
energy for the individual but they permit him to
see things only from their fixed predetermined
angle. What opportunity, for example, has the
child reared in an orthodox Protestant home for
gaining any true historical appreciation of the
Pope, Jesus of Nazareth, the Devil, or Voltaire?
The very definiteness, the fixity and finality of
those mental stereotypes called Fundamentalist
theology, ought to arouse all the more serious mis-
givings as to their trustworthiness as infallible

guides through that vast and uncharted realm of God and sin and heaven and hell.

Since we must have stereotypes and since they are a 'manifest source of danger to the integrity of our mental lives it would appear that the only wise course is to use our stereotypes with the constant realization of the fact that they are after all merely mental pictures. This would imply more or less of a critical attitude towards the pictures we carry around in our heads about men and things. It would emancipate us from the tyranny of the stereotyped attitudes that we inherit in religion, politics, business, and morals. As an inevitable result of this critical attitude men would be inclined to be more tolerant of those who differ with them. For, after all, differences between Catholic and Protestant, native American and foreigner, laborer and capitalist, resolve themselves back into stereotypes that are indigenous to each group or class and which the member of that class has absorbed under the conviction that they are ultimate and absolute truth. If we approach our stereotypes in this critical and tolerant attitude their use will be found to be thoroughly justifiable and even indispensable. But our stereotypes should at all times be our mental servants and never our intellectual tyrants.

The man who surrenders abjectly to the mental stereotypes of his church, party, business, community, nation, or race permits himself to be branded like a sheep and should realize that in time like a sheep he will either be sheared or slaughtered.

V

Last but not least in our analysis of the Klan psychology comes the part played by the feelings aroused by the war. We all feel strongly about all matters which we consider of vital importance. Religion, for example, which has to do with the supreme values of life, arouses the noblest enthusiasms of men. Those sentiments built up around country, church, home, are always strongly tinged with emotion because they deal with important segments of our lives. When the course of our lives runs smoothly these emotions are not strongly in evidence for the simple reason that situations are lacking which call them into play. A mother's love for her child is most in evidence when the child is in danger. The ecclesiastic's love for his church is most in evidence when he thinks its doctrines are menaced. The patriot's love for his country is most in evidence when it is

endangered by war. That is to say, all disturbed
social situations such as those created by war or
revolution are always situations in which the atmosphere is tense with emotions. It follows, therefore, that periods of profound disturbance, times
when the very foundations of society are shaken,
when men feel themselves in danger of losing
their grip upon fundamental loyalties, when the
pole-stars are being blotted from their skies in religion, politics, or morals, are the periods in the
history of society when men are more apt to be
guided by their feelings than by reason. For it is
then that our vague emotional attitudes usually
organized and rationalized by a fixed framework
of ideas, as in authoritative creeds or established
ways of life, are set free, precipitated as it were
in the social solution, because the normal setting
in which these emotions function is destroyed or
seriously deranged.

The Klan, though organized in 1915, owes its
marvellous growth to the disturbed post-war conditions. The war, with its hymns of hate, its stories of poison gas and human carnage, its secret
spyings upon fellow Americans, its accounts of
Belgian atrocities, its imprisonment of radicals,
its fearful tales of Bolshevist designs upon American institutions, had opened up the fountains of

the great deep of national feeling. After the armistice these hates kindled by the war and to which the nation had become habituated during years of bloodshed were suddenly set adrift because stripped of the objects and the ends around which they had been organized by the experience of the war. As a nation we had cultivated a taste for the cruel, the brutal, the intolerant, and the un-Christian that demanded gratification. Here was an unparalleled opportunity for the Klan "salesmen of hate." The Klan offered just what the war-torn distraught emotions of the nation demanded.

The Klan has literally battened upon the irrational fear psychology that followed on the heels of the war. The Klan's first move in the South was to capitalize the white's fear of the Negro owing to the Negro's new ambitions created by his fight for democracy and the increased demands for his labor. To-day, for various reasons, the Negro is a negligible quantity in the Klan issue South or North. The center of the fear psychology has been shifted even in the South from the Negro to the Catholic, the Jew, and the foreigner. What keeps the Klan alive in the face of powerful opposition and its patent incompatibility with the principles of true Americanism is undoubtedly a widespread distrust of all things foreign.

The peak of this wave of antagonism to all things foreign was reached in 1920 when the Klan began to grow by leaps and bounds. This fear of alien influence did much to defeat the strenuous efforts during the campaign of 1920 to induce this country to become a member of the League of Nations. The campaign itself was one dominated not so much by reason and the genuine merits of the issue as by blind emotions. The leaders of the opposition to Wilson's policies often strengthened these fears by demagogic appeals to the fear of entangling foreign alliances ingrained in the average American. The defeat of Wilson and his League was mainly the result of an emotional upheaval. It was the product of a fear psychology not unmixed with more unworthy emotions.

This fear psychology has registered itself in a radical and apparently irrational change in our immigration policy. Almost half a century ago writers and investigators had been asserting that the native American was voluntarily eliminating himself and his descendants by his immigration policy. Sober statistics have long been available to show that through its immigration policy the nation has been assiduously creating a situation by which in time the reins of power, politically, economically, and religiously, would pass from the scions of the old stock to the children of the alien. But the politicians jockeyed for spoils and power and the native American chased the dollar while millions of alien and often inferior stock flooded our shores. Suddenly, almost over night, Congress passed a law which for its drastic modification of policy is perhaps without a parallel in our political history. Here we have the result not of sober reason nor of a well-matured and thought-out national policy but of fear psychology. The immense popularity of this drastic immigration law with the masses of Americans should throw some light for us upon the readiness with which men listen to the Klan's anti-foreign propaganda.

This fear psychology explains the effective use by the Klan of anti-Semitism and anti-Catholicism. The Catholic Church has never been a menace to the political, moral, or religious integrity of the nation. The members of the Roman Catholic communion are to-day more enlightened, wealthier, and more closely identified with the life of the nation than ever before. From the Catholic Church have always come and are now coming in increasing numbers many of the most intelligent and patriotic members of our citizenship. The

Catholic Church, however, thanks to its hierarchical organization centering in Rome and thanks to its super-nationalism with its assumption of a spiritual and moral sovereignty that claims to be superior to that of American society, lays itself open to the charge of being undemocratic, alien, un-American. Hence the Roman Catholic Church has become the victim of the fear of alien influence in America. The Jew, who has recently been coming to this country mainly from Russia and Southeastern Europe by hundreds of thousands and who, true to his urban traits, has crowded into New York and other large cities where his alien characteristics are thrust into the face of the native American on the street, in the hotel or department store, has also come in for his share of the prevalent fear psychology. Henry Ford in the anti-Semitic publication he has fathered, *The International Jew*, has voiced the fears of the native American brought into close contact with the unassimilated and disagreeably alien Jewish population of our large centers. The Klan has simply capitalized this situation with tremendous success.

CHAPTER V

THE KLAN AND NATIVISM

THE enumerations of the objectives of the Klan, no matter from what section of the country they come, usually include the phrase "one hundred percent Americanism." There is, of course, the utmost vagueness among Klansmen themselves as to the meaning of this term. If, however, there is one central idea that serves to unify this vast, inchoate Klan movement, sprawling over the land like pent-up waters suddenly set free, it must be sought in this phrase "one hundred percent Americanism." Americanism as it falls from the lips of the Klansman is synonymous with Nativism. That is to say, one hundred per cent Americanism is identified in the mind of the Klansman with a body of religious, political, economic, and social traditions indigenous to the original American stock and their descendants. The Klan thrives best in those communities where this old American stock has escaped the influence of the immigrant waves on the one hand and of indus-

127

trialism on the other. There is a larger percentage of the old undiluted American stock in the
South and Southwest and in Oregon than in any
other section of the country. This stock is also
much in evidence throughout the Middle West. In
all these regions the Klan has flourished like the
proverbial green bay tree. On the other hand,
the Klan has found a cold reception in our large
cities and in the great manufacturing centers with
their welter of immigrant groups, their dearth
of social traditions, and their impersonal pecun-
iary measure of values. The Klan, in its last
analysis, is a protest on the part of this old American stock against the forces which for good or
ill are transforming American society. It is essentially conservative and harks back in politics,
in religion, and in social ethics to the traditions
of the fathers. It is but the latest phase of what
for the lack of a better term we shall call Nativism.

I

Nativism or Native Americanism is a movement which has manifested itself in varying
forms and with varying intensity for almost one
hundred years. It originated as a movement
of self-defence on the part of the older native

stock threatened with submergence by the re-
current waves of immigration. It will be found
that the outbursts of Nativism are always con-
comitants of an immigrant wave. There have
been four great waves of immigration into this
country. The first stretched approximately from
1831 to 1861, reaching its peak in 1855. During
these three decades some four millions of foreigners were added to our population. The second
wave extended from 1862 to 1877, reaching its
peak in 1873. From 1831 to 1877 the immigrants
came principally from the British Isles and Germany. The third great immigrant wave extended
from 1878 to 1897, reaching its peak in 1882. This
wave added something like nine millions to our
population, Germans and British subjects still
predominating though the immigrant tides from
Italy, Austria-Hungary, and Russia were getting
under way.

The fourth and last immigrant wave extended
from 1898 to the outbreak of the war and was
marked by two peak years. In 1907 immigration
reached the astounding figure of 1,285,349, only
a few thousand more than the 1,218,480 who
arrived in 1913. During this period Italy took
the lead, followed closely by Austria-Hungary
and Russia while Germany and the British Isles

trailed far behind. During six of these fourteen years the immigrant host numbered over one
million annually, the total being over fourteen
millions for the period. The total number of immigrants to this country since 1820, when reliable
data began to be kept, is over thirty-three millions.
These to-day together with their descendants outnumber the descendants of the old Colonial stock.
According to a conservative estimate some forty
millions or perhaps forty-two percent of the white
population of this country are descended through
both parents from the old Colonial stock. It is
from this stock that the various forms of the Nativist movement, including its latest manifestation, the Ku Klux Klan, have drawn their chief
support.

As was to be expected, the Nativist movements
manifested themselves just after the peak had
been reached in each of the great immigrant
waves. Know-Nothingism, for example, which
was the first pronounced manifestation of Nativism, was at its height in 1855, the year after
the first great immigrant wave reached its
peak. Sporadic Nativist societies had begun to
appear prior to Know-Nothingism, such as the
Patriotic Sons of America, founded in Philadel-
phia in 1847 just when the first immigrant wave

was beginning to mount high and reorganized in 1866 when the second immigrant wave was coming on. It sought to inculcate pure Americanism by opposing all foreign influence, by insisting upon the separation of church and state, by keeping public schools free from ecclesiastical influence and by requiring longer residence of foreigners before admission to citizenship. This has remained the general platform of all subsequent Nativist organizations. The peak year of the second wave was 1873, the effect of which was seen in the planks introduced into Republican and Democratic platforms in 1876 in support of Nativism, the Republican plank going so far as to recommend a constitutional amendment preventing the use of public funds or property in support of sectarian schools.

The third peak of immigration was reached in 1882 with a slightly lesser peak in 1892. During this period Nativism asserted itself in the American Protective Association organized in 1887 and attaining greatest popularity in 1894 and 1895, thus faithfully registering the psychological effect of the peak year 1892. There were numerous other Nativist societies founded about the same time, the next in importance to the A. P. A. being the National League for the Protection of

American Institutions, which numbered among its members some of the most prominent men of the time. The peak of the fourth and last immigrant wave was 1907 with a slightly lesser peak in 1914. The Klan was organized in 1915. The modern Ku Klux Klan was not strictly speaking the immediate product of Nativism, being Southern and sectional in origin. But the Klan, thanks to the skill of the promoter, E. Y. Clarke, and the fear of alien influences aroused by the war, has become a national movement mainly because it has tapped this old stream of Nativist traditions. For this reason the modern Klan, so far as its main idea is concerned, is a lineal descendant of Know-Nothingism and the American Protective Association. This, rather than its connections with the old Klan of Reconstruction days, is responsible for the powerful appeal the Klan has made to Americans in every part of the country. This is the bond that unites Klansmen from such widely divergent sections as Maine and Texas, Ohio and Georgia, Oklahoma and New Jersey, Oregon and Indiana.

II

To understand the Klan, then, we must understand what is meant by Nativism. Perhaps the earliest formulation of the principles of Nativism is to be found in the literature of the Know-Nothings, a term supposed to be derived from the reply the members of this secret oath-bound organization gave to inquiries about the order by outsiders. Originating in New York State in 1852 as a secret society with oath, passwords, grip, and ritual, the Know-Nothings spread rapidly and by 1854 began to play a part in politics. Under the pressure of political ambitions the secret machinery was later dropped and they appeared as the American Party, though the soubriquet Know-Nothings still clung to them. The chief reason for the rise of Know-Nothingism was the political situation created by the sudden flood of immigrants who had easy access to the franchise, for the proper exercise of which, however, they were not qualified either mentally or morally. Where the old parties were evenly balanced it was often possible for this foreign group to wield the actual balance of power. Their votes were eagerly sought by the politicians, and when these votes brought political success the new Americans demanded their share of the spoils. As a result, "The American people," says a Know-Nothing writer, "have found themselves in the power of alien-born men, most of them ignorant, many brutish, a portion of whom can neither read nor write, and who have not been in the country long enough to learn anything of its institutions or to imbibe a genuine American sentiment. They are in no sense or degree Americans, except as occupants of American soil. In character, education, if they have any, habits, modes of thinking, social and religious sentiments, and in every endowment of birth and culture, they are *foreign* and to a great extent *anti*-American." Out of this exigency arose the American Party. It was born of the instinct of self-preservation. It was felt that the old parties were impotent to give relief. The fundamental political dogma of the American Party and of Nativism is that *"Americans shall govern America."*

Closely connected with this first thesis of Nativism, namely, America for Americans, we have another scarcely less important and that is the maintenance of the Protestant faith. "The entire creed [of Know-Nothingism] we think is comprised in these two words—Americanism and Protestantism," says a Know-Nothing authority. The two are not to be separated. Protestantism is but the religious phase of Americanism. Nativism took on this politico-religious form owing to the pressure of the Roman Catholic Church.

The new Americans were predominantly Catholic. It was claimed that the Catholic Church gained through them a strategic position by which it was able to shape public policies. Protestantism was thrust into the background because the politician could not assert the traditional rights of Protestantism as the original national faith without danger of losing Catholic votes. It appeared to the Know-Nothings, therefore, that "the two great parties and the federal government were bound hand and foot to the chair of the Roman Pontiff, so far as their Protestantism was concerned." The Know-Nothing party owed its remarkable spread, just as does the Klan, to the fact that it provided a means of political expression for this native Protestantism disgruntled and alarmed by the spread of Catholicism.

The Know-Nothings contended, as does the Klan, that this emphasis of Protestantism was not a surrender of the American doctrine of the separation of church and state. "It is only the political element of Protestantism which they make use of. The Protestant faith as derived from the Bible for the use of the soul is one thing; and Protestantism as a political element of the state, which ordains that every man shall be permitted to read and interpret the Bible for him-

self and not be forced to receive and believe only
what the priest prescribes and orders, is another.
This political element of Protestantism is essential both to civil and religious freedom; and the
latter can only be secured by the former.'' That
is to say, it is the political philosophy of American Protestantism that is at stake. Nativism will
see that ''all the civil rights of Papists will be respected and their religion, as a private right, and
for all lawful purposes, as of religious societies,
will be vindicated from insult.'' But while ''the
American Party asks no favor of Papists and ex-
pects none, they intend as Protestants to govern
the country without their aid or hindrance.''
Here we have, clearly stated three quarters of a
century ago, the contentions of the Klan with regard to Catholicism and the Protestant faith.
Protestantism is civilly and politically a constitu-
ent element in Americanism. Catholicism, owing
to the fact that its genius does not permit the separation of church and state, is inimical to true
Americanism—such was and still remains the contention of Nativism.

The Nativist movement later registered itself
in the organization of various anti-Catholic societies, the most numerous and powerful of which
was the American Protective Association and the

most respectable the National League for the Protection of American Institutions. The latter was a non-secret patriotic organization whose first president was John Jay with William Strong, ex-Justice of the Supreme Court, as vice-president. Among its membership were such prominent men as William Fellowes Morgan, General Francis Walker, Judge Peckham, afterwards appointed to the Supreme Bench by President Cleveland, Henry Hitchcock, ex-president of the American Bar, President Andrews of Brown, President Jordan of Stanford, President Rogers of Northwestern, Levi P. Morton, Cornelius Bliss, Matthew Hale, J. Pierpont Morgan, Cornelius Vanderbilt, Charles Scribner, Cyrus W. Field, and Rutherford B. Hayes. It thus explains the reason for its existence. "A movement, with audacious demands and specious claims, has been initiated in the state of New York for the division of the public school funds on sectarian lines and it is announced that the same program is proposed for all the states. That this has mainly in view selfish and not public ends is shown by the fact that the movement is being pushed almost exclusively by a single religious denomination which for many years by its chief authorities has been assaulting the public school system." The organization sought to safe-

guard native Americanism through the adoption
of an amendment to the Constitution against sectarian interference with the public schools. While
its immediate object was not attained, the League
exercised wide influence and aided in the insertion
into different state constitutions of laws designed
to preserve the integrity of the public school system.

The American Protective Association, which is
not to be confused with the National League for
the Protection of American Institutions, was especially strong in the Middle West, just where
the Klan numbers its largest membership to-day,
and at one time claimed a membership of over
two millions. The A. P. A. was a secret, oath-
bound organization which was opposed to Catholicism in every shape or form. The A. P. A. is
the real connecting link between the Klan and
Know-Nothingism. The accounts of the methods
of the A. P. A. might easily be mistaken for accounts of the Klan. The A. P. A. made effective
use of certain campaign documents such as a leaf-
let entitled "Instructions to Catholics" purport-
ing to be a platform for a Papal Party, "decreed
and ordered by the provincial council at their ses-
sion, August 5, 1890" and bearing the signatures
of eight archbishops and the counter-signature of

Cardinal Gibbons. In this curious document these Catholic authorities are made to "view with alarm" the spread of education, the diffusion of the English language, and the teaching of the young to think; they oppose the public schools as godless and seek to control municipal governments, railroads, manufactories, mines, and especially the press. To accomplish these ends it may prove necessary "to remove or crowd out the American heretics who are now employed."

A second document used as anti-Catholic propaganda was a pseudo-encyclical of Pope Leo XIII, dated December 25th, 1891, in which the Pope is made to assert that the American continent belongs to him and his church by virtue of its discovery by a Catholic, Columbus, and that the time is soon coming when he will take forcible possession, at which time "it will be the duty of the faithful to exterminate all heretics found within the jurisdiction of the United States." There is reason to believe that some of the anti-Catholic literature used by the A. P. A. has been revived and utilized by the Klan. Certainly the Klan has made most effective use of the blood-curdling oath of the Knights of Columbus long shown to be a forgery. Throughout the Middle West Klan solicitors are provided with a booklet, "Making

America Catholic,'' compiled by A. H. Beach and
published in 1922. It consists of quotations, rather cleverly arranged and given without comment, from papal encyclicals, decrees of councils,
Catholic books and periodicals, the utterances of
priests, bishops, archbishops, and cardinals, all
designed to show the fundamental antagonism of
Catholicism to American institutions and traditions.

III

In any fair estimate of the Nativist movement
to which the Klan belongs, it must be freely
granted that the original American stock has a
very real grievance. The virtues, real or imagined,
of this old American stock have provided the poet,
the romancer, and the political spellbinder with
grateful themes while in actual reality this old
stock has been sadly discriminated against. It
has always been a popular belief that every immigrant means a pure gain in population. That is to
say, immigration is popularly supposed to con-
tribute an increase in the population of the country over and above the normal increase due to
the natural functioning of the reproductive powers
of the original American stock. On this assumption the population of the country to-day is sup-

posed to consist of that number of the descendants of the original stock of Colonial times who would have been born had there been no great immigrant waves, plus the immigrants and their descendants. This is in all probability an unwarranted assumption. There are good grounds for the contention that the millions who have swarmed to our shores do not represent actual gains in our population. They have simply taken the place of the natural increase of the original stock which would have occurred had there been no immigration. Every immigrant, therefore, merely supplants a possible son or daughter of the old American stock. Immigration, in other words, has thus acted as a serious check upon the perpetuation of the original stock.

It is argued in support of this thesis that the natural increase of the original American stock before the coming of the immigrant was very great, mounting from four millions in 1790 to thirteen millions in 1830, an increase of 227 percent in four decades. Had this increase continued, the population of this country would have been over one hundred millions in 1900 instead of seventy-six millions, the actual number, which included millions of immigrants. It is interesting to note, furthermore, that the decline in the birth-rate of the original stock began just as the pressure of the immigrants began to be felt and was most pronounced in those sections of the country, such as New England, where the immigrants were most in evidence. To these general observations must be added the Malthusian principle, which has never been invalidated, namely, that increase of population always tends to adjust itself to the means of subsistence. Given the means of subsistence at a certain stage in the history of the American nation and given a certain addition to the population through immigration at that stage, it is contended that this increase restricts by so much the possible increase of the original American stock.

A most striking illustration of this Malthusian law is found in the disastrous effects upon the original American stock of the competition between its standard of living and that of the immigrant. The standard of living, a comprehensive term for those necessities, conventions, luxuries, or what not, which a given group deems necessary for the maintenance of its social status, is much higher in the case of the native American than in that of the immigrant. The native American, forced to compete with the lower wage and lower standard of living of the immigrant, is faced with the alternatives of limiting the size of his family or of lowering his standard of living. He elects invariably the former, thus committing himself to a policy of race suicide. Time might equalize this competition, since the immigrant tends to limit his family also as he approximates the American standard of living, but for the fact that decrease in the births of native children creates a constant demand for cheap and abundant alien labor which the American market cannot supply. The net result has been the development of an industrial order dependent for its profits upon unrestricted immigration. In his zeal for profits the short-sighted native American's policy meant the slow but inevitable elimination of his group.

IV

All Nativists, including the Klan, consider themselves the sole proprietors of Americanism. They tell us it was the forbears of the native Americans who acquired at the cost of much blood and suffering the freedom and independence of this country and bequeathed this legacy to their sons. "The alien born has no property in them, except by adoption," says a Know-Nothing writer. "With him it is not an inheritance but a gift. There is no law of nature or of nations by which the alien born can lay claim to such property. If it is of sufficient value to be sought by the alien, it is doubtless of sufficient value for the owners to prescribe the terms of acquisition." This amounts to a claim of a monopoly of American traditions on the part of the Nativists.

To examine critically the justification for the claims of the Nativist raises at once the much debated question, "What is Americanism?" Generally speaking, there are two answers to this question. One is what may be called the humanitarian and idealistic doctrine that Americanism is a body of ideals or, if you please, a mental attitude which may be attained independent of race, cultural background, or continuity of social heritage. This humanitarian and idealistic position has drawn its support from the fact that American political ideals have always had a detached existence more or less remote from political realities, from the struggle to free the slave and endow him with complete American citizenship, from the economic need for cheap labor, and finally from the traditional belief that America was intended by God to be the asylum of the oppressed of all nations. The other conception of Americanism is that of the Nativist who contends that national ideals cannot be divorced from ethnic stock, language, laws, religion, and continuity of social traditions. Nativism contains, implicitly at least, the assumption that a nation, like an individual, is a psycho-physical organism. Ideas, sentiments, loyalties, do not thrive as sublimated spiritual abstractions. They are the correlatives in the realm of thought and feeling of prevailing ways of life in business, politics, and social relations. Destroy or seriously disrupt this material basis of these ideas through revolution, through war, or through vast and sudden shifts in the ethnic composition of society, and you endanger these ideals. The contention of Nativism and the Klan is that the group it represents, by virtue of its ethnic homogeneity, its close and constant identification with the evolution of American society, is best equipped to be the guardian of American traditions. The claim is one that can not be lightly dismissed or ignored.

V

There are at least three arguments Nativists may advance in support of their contention that the old stock must control and direct national life. Nativists may base their claim upon the alleged

inherent superiority of the original racial stock
that established American institutions, upon the
possession of superior education and intelligence
so necessary for the solution of present-day
problems, or upon the fact that the scions of the
old stock occupy among the classes and groups in
society a mediating position which entitles them
to play the leading part in the formation of public
opinion, the final arbiter of issues in a democracy.

Since the great war our book stalls have been
flooded with hectic works that have come to the
support of Native Americanism from the stand-
point of race. They are for the most part glorifi-
cations of the Nordic race. One of the more recent of these writers thus states the conclusion
of his argument: "Would it not be wise for us to
consider carefully our country's present situation? Events have occurred which would have
seemed to our forefathers impossible. Doctrines
have been widely preached subversive of their institutions, and this has been accomplished by
methods too contemptible and too base to be
cited here. Americans of the old stock have still
left some rights, are still entitled to some consideration, and, failing to receive it, still hold in their
hands the power to enforce respect and obedience
to the institutions they love. Never yet have they

failed to carry any great cause which they have es-
poused. The old American blood once roused can
still be counted upon absolutely. . . . It was not
the Russian, nor the Pole, nor any other foreign
element who, roused by infamous cruelties, swept
the country into the Spanish War. It was not the
Russian, nor the Pole, nor any other foreign strain
who swept the country into this last war,—it was
the old American stock which has ever stood for
right and justice." (Charles W. Gould, *America
a Family Matter*, p. 159f. Similar ideas are advanced by William McDougall, *Is America Safe
for Democracy?* Lothrop Stoddard, *The Rising
Tide of Color;* Madison Grant, *The Passing of a
Great Race.*) This is the familiar language of
Nativism, and the large reading public these books
have found should throw some light for us upon
the spread of the Klan.

There is much that seems to support the Nativist claim to supremacy based upon racial stock.
There is first the indisputable fact of the relative
ethnic homogeneity of the American stock at the
time of the Revolution when this old stock shaped
our national institutions. Old New England with
a pure English stock left a deep impress upon the
nation while modern New England with a diverse
ethnic stock is now playing a lame and impo-

tent rôle in the life of the nation. Granting the
contention of the Nativist as to the superiority of
this original stock, who is responsible for the present situation? This same splendid original American stock has encouraged an immigration policy
by which of its own free will it has doomed itself to
the position of a racial minority. For good or for
ill the days of the racial predominance of the
Colonial stock are gone, and apparently forever.
The racial unity of the American nation now belongs to the past. What the outcome of our racial "melting pot" will be rests upon the knees of
the gods. It may very well be, as is asserted of
the racial potpourri in Brazil and other lands to
the south of us, that some racial type, perhaps
that of the original American stock, will prevail,
impressing itself upon all the other racial variants.
It may, be as Zangwill makes his hero, the
Russian Jew, say in the *Melting Pot*, "America is
God's Crucible, the great Melting Pot where all
the races of Europe are melting and re-forming.
. . . The real American has not yet arrived. He
is only in the Crucible. I tell you—he will be the
fusion of all races, perhaps the coming Super-
man."

At the present stage of national development
the pressing problem is, what shall be the rela-

tions of these various ethnic groups to each other? Shall we encourage, in the interest of effective social control, the dominance of one group, such as the descendants of the old stock, shall we seek a federation of racial groups, or shall we with the sentimental idealists ignore race as a negligible factor in the problem? Without in the least minimizing race as a factor in the situation it is safe to say that race alone can never be made the basis for a valid claim to leadership in a democracy. The possession of a white skin does not predestine a man to mastery any more than the possession of a black skin predestines him to slavery. The Klan contention of "white supremacy," in so far as it is based upon the mere accident of skin-color, is the sheerest democratic heresy. Meanwhile, it is worthy of note that, while the champion of the old American stock is uncritically assuming the correctness of his theory of Americanism and is seeking to convince recalcitrants by Lusk laws or tar and feather parties, some of the most scholarly contributions to the problem are being made by Americans of alien stock whose conclusions are uniformly opposed to the orthodox one hundred percent Americanism of the Nativists. (See, for example, I. B. Berkson: *Theories of Americanization,* 1920.)

Recently an interesting plea has been made for the leadership of the descendants of the old American stock on the ground that they furnish the brain power of the nation. (John Corbin, *The Return of the Middle Class,* 1923.) American society, it is contended, is divided into three major classes, those who work with their hands, those who work with their brains, and the capitalists. The energies of the hand-worker are absorbed by the struggle for bread, those of the capitalist by the struggle for profits, while the brain workers alone, who include the intellectual and professional classes, are in the position to play a rôle of real leadership. These brain-workers are "very largely" the descendants of the original American stock. They, together with the kindred immigrants of Nordic stock coming from northern Europe, compose three-fourths of our population and are best equipped, we are told, by virtue of their native ability to provide national leadership. Upon closer scrutiny it would appear that this argument resolves itself into a variant of the racialists' theory that the original American stock and its descendants owe their brains and hence their right to leadership not to the social or cultural advantages which they enjoy but to the inherent superiority of their racial stock. Incidentally, it may be remarked that this threefold classification of society is so vague as to be of little practical value. The term "brain-workers" cuts across more than it follows actual social stratifications and groupings.

It is possible for the Nativists to build up a much stronger argument in support of their bid for supremacy by claiming that their group furnishes the best basis for a saving middle class in American society. In every society there must be a ruling class or at least a class that forms the basis for social control. The free citizens of ancient Athens, the patricians of Rome, the clergy of the Middle Ages, the bourgeoisie of early nineteenth-century France and England, the Junkers of pre-war Germany, the slavocracy of the antebellum South, the Captains of Industry two or three decades ago—all these served in more or less pronounced fashion as agents of social control in the societies of which they were members. This is more or less inevitable, for every social order must have direction and purpose. There must be individuals and groups through whom social unity is secured. Government is and always will be more or less the expression of the will of a class. The problem is not so much one of getting rid of a ruling class as of making sure that the class which dominates furthers the good of the whole. Democracies are no exception to this general rule. They, too, must have their ruling class. In theory, if not in actual practice, the ruling class in modern democracies has been the so-called middle or mediating class. The idea seems to have been suggested by the rôle played by the bourgeoisie in the formation of nineteenth-century democracy in France, England, and America.

The chief justification of the rule of the middle class in a democracy lies in the important rôle this class is supposed to play in the formation of public opinion. In a democracy sovereignty is vested in no one individual or group. The real sovereign is reason or public opinion. But public opinion is not an individual affair; it is a social product. The reasoned common sense of the community is theoretically the real ruler in a democracy. While this reasoned common sense is the sole possession of no individual or class, any class which by training or social position is best equipped to express this reasoned common sense and put it into execution must necessarily take precedence over other classes. The middle class, at least from the point of view of traditional nineteenth-century democracy, is entitled to precedence because it, more than any other class, gives shape to public opinion.

In order adequately to perform its task of molding opinion the middle class must have certain qualities. It must be composed mainly of those who are neither very poor nor very rich. The middle class must be free from poverty because poverty is a form of slavery and prevents the individual or the group from entering wholeheartedly and sympathetically into the life of the community. A measure of economic goods also permits leisure for reflection and the effective discharge of social and political duties. On the other hand, the middle class must know the discipline of work to understand the life of the workers and to escape the social isolation and artificial conceptions of life too often the bane of the very rich. The middle class must be informed. That is to say, it must have a keen intellectual appreciation of the drift of things in society and be endowed with a measure of critical independence of mind if it is to perform properly its exceedingly important task of giving shape to public opinion. The formation of effective public opinion involves the reduction to intelligible terms of that vast mass of class passions and prejudices, local loves and hates, the crude unreasoned loyalties that jostle each other in the welter of immediate social experience. This is no easy task but it is the condition prerequisite to effective leadership in a democracy. Finally the middle class must be class-conscious in the sense that it must be aware of its own existence and of its peculiar tasks. It goes without saying that effective class-consciousness is never gained except through the spur and discipline of action. It is only while performing some common social task and thereby experiencing the psychological effects of group action that any class becomes aware of its own existence and formulates its ends.

To what extent does the Klan measure up to those things required of the class that aspires to leadership in American democracy? Does it represent an intelligent, class-conscious, sanely balanced middle class to which may be entrusted the most important task of molding public sentiment? In the first place, it must be acknowledged that the Klan draws its support mainly from the old American stock which by tradition and training occupies a strategic position in American society. This old stock may well claim that it can furnish us with the best basis for a democratic ruling middle class. Assuming, however, that such a middle class is possible to-day in American society, an assumption which, to say the least, is debatable, the Klan includes only a minority of those who are supposed to make up this middle class. As we have seen, there are large segments of American society, composed of descendants of native American stock, who do not sympathize with the Klan. The Klan does not speak for this group as a whole. The Klan speaks mainly for that provincial, small-town, native Americanism which is intensely suspicious of all things foreign. The Klan, furthermore, does not strive to mediate between conflicting groups and classes. It is intensely and bitterly partisan. It does not seek to cultivate the whole or social point of view. The Klan's intolerance incapacitates it for the task of molding public opinion.

Finally, does the Klan measure up to the intellectual requirements of the dominant middle class? If there is one outstanding fact to be noted of the majority of the Klan members it is their intellectual mediocrity. Neither the intellectual leaders of the community nor the men of ability in the professions or business tend to identify themselves with the Klan. A long-time resident of Atlanta who has observed the Klan at close range makes this observation, "The Ku Klux Klan, so far as my observation goes, is composed principally of politicians and that class of men who earn twenty, twenty-five, or thirty dollars per week. In other words, the average intelligence of the membership would be low. Where an intelligent man has become a member of the order it is because that man is unscrupulous and is using the order to enhance his own interests politically or otherwise. . . . They do a lot of talking about their ideals but they do nothing so far as I can see except talk. That, I believe, is because they do not have members of sufficient brains or vision to really do anything along these lines." This statement is somewhat extreme but it has back of it a substantial basis of truth. The Klan is conspicuously lacking in that refinement of sentiment and critical independence of thought which must be possessed by any individual or class that undertakes to shape public opinion in a democracy.

CHAPTER VI

THE KLAN AND ANTI-CATHOLICISM

I

THROUGH a questionnaire, by personal interviews and otherwise, the writer has attempted to discover the reasons for joining the Klan. Naturally one finds the greatest variety of motives, religious, racial, social, political, commercial, but the motive which has gained most members for the Klan, taking precedence over all others in the strength and universality of its appeal, is undoubtedly anti-Catholicism. Out of several hundred representative citizens from various parts of the country who were asked to mention, in the order of the effectiveness of their appeal, the incentives to join the Klan, all mentioned anti-Catholicism and a large percentage placed it first. This anti-Catholicism is not localized, being strong in Pennsylvania, Indiana, Kansas, Oregon, as well as in Georgia and Louisiana. Furthermore, it is insisted that this anti-Catholicism is not to be identified with mere religious prejudice. Klansmen reiterate that they are not opposed to Catholicism as a religion. They acknowledge freely the right of the Catholic to worship God according to the dictates of his own conscience. There are of course surface irritants such as the petty jealousy and fear the Protestant clergy and laity often show for the power and prestige of the Church of Rome, the reputed clannishness of the Catholics, the charges of collusion between priest and politician to get social control, and the alleged hostility of Catholics to the public school. But deeper than all this lies the vague feeling that the center of authority of the Roman Catholic Church, as opposed to Protestantism, lies outside of and superior to the American society in which Catholic and Protestant live. The Klan interprets this as a menace to the spiritual and moral integrity of America. It is asserted that for one very large group, namely, the Catholics, the enlightened moral and religious sensibilities of the American people cannot speak the last word. That last word is spoken by the infallible head of a vast theocratic autocracy, namely, the Pope. There is not the slightest doubt that this has gained for the Klan more serious-minded supporters, North, South, East, and West, than anything else. As a prominent Texan, not a Klansman, puts it, "The popular idea is that the Klan is loyal to our government and many organizations are not. It is not religion in the Romanist to which the Klan objects, but treason." Such an accusation sounds harsh and unjust. We are not concerned now to discuss its justification. The significant thing to remember here is that this attitude is taken towards the Roman Catholic Church by millions of Americans, many of whom have no connection with the Klan.

What is the attitude of the twenty millions of Catholic Americans towards the Klan? There exists for the Catholic of course the very evident temptation of being drawn into a fruitless and undignified squabble with the Klan. It is possible that Catholic support, financial and moral, is behind the American Unity League of Chicago organized to fight the Klan. The League's official organ, *Tolerance*, may be said to rival the most rabid Klan publications in its shrieking and hysterical condemnations of all things pertaining to the Klan. At the meetings of the League, speakers indulge in passionate oratory, consisting for the most part of denunciations of the Klan mingled with the insistence upon "rights" of Irish-Catholic, Jew, or Negro, while, as a Chicago paper remarked, "No one seems to be interested in protecting the rights of those who call themselves plain, ordinary American citizens." On the whole, however, it must be said that the Catholic group, especially the official representatives of the Catholic Church, have conducted themselves with a dignity and reserve that stand in pleasing contrast to the hectic abandon of the leaders of the Klan.

In no state of the union perhaps has the antagonism between Protestant and Catholic been fanned by the Klan to such a dangerous pitch as in Louisiana during the Mer Rouge trials and the subsequent political campaigns. In the town of Lafayette, in southern Louisiana, largely Catholic, feeling ran so strong in March, 1923, due to the publication of the list of charter members of the Klan, that there was great danger of bloodshed. The Catholic bishop, Rev. Jules B. Jeanmard, issued a proclamation deploring a situation that threatened the "total disruption of that spirit of harmony, tolerance and brotherly love that has characterized our community heretofore" and reminding his people that they were "too big, too generous and brave" to take advantage of their numerical superiority to wreak a cheap revenge upon the Klan. Bishop Jeanmard undoubtedly

voices the feeling of all enlightened Catholics
when he asserts that the Klan "uses the language
of the Ghetto in speaking of persons and things
Catholics hold sacred and impugns our loyalty and
devotion to the country and its institutions." A
prominent Catholic of Evansville, Indiana, writes,
"Catholics without exception condemn the Klan
as un-American and un-Christian, violating in
particular the laws of charity and dangerous to
democratic government."

II

An historian of the Know-Nothing Party asserted that this party owed its vitality to "the time-
honored Anglo-Saxon and Evangelical aspersion
of the integrity of Catholic citizenship, an aspersion as old as the age of Queen Elizabeth and
responsible for the persecuting statutes of her
time; an aspersion too, which though diminishing
in force from generation to generation is, nevertheless, liable to recur in years to come and during future flurries of intolerance" (Humphrey J.
Desmond, *The Know-Nothing Party*, p. 109). If
the historian had written with prophetic knowledge of the rise of the modern Ku Klux Klan he
could not have forecast the future more ac-

curately. The antipathy of the Klansman to the
Catholic is therefore nothing new. It is but the
latest phase of a mental attitude that has characterized native Americanism from the very beginning. Obviously, then, we can best grasp the
meaning of the present anti-Catholic outburst in
the light of the historical perspective.

We have seen that the Nativist movement stimu-
lated by the first two great immigrant tides whose
peak years were 1854 and 1872 was primarily
political and only secondarily religious. The religious phase was present in the case of Know-
Nothingism but grew out of the political. The
Nativist opposition aroused by the third immigrant wave of 1894, however, and represented by
the American Protective Association (A. P. A.)
was mainly religious. The emphasis of the religious phase of Nativism in the early nineties
was due to the sudden rise to a position of commanding influence in almost every phase of American life of the Roman Catholic Church. From 1880
to 1894 over eight millions of immigrants arrived,
the majority of whom were Catholics. These, together with the large Catholic additions of the
first two waves of immigration, increased the
Catholic element so rapidly as to cause great un-
easiness among the Nativists. The Catholics in

1840 numbered little more than a million. In 1895 Catholic authorities claimed 12,500,000 followers of the Catholic faith. The yearly increase of the Catholic population, which in 1850 was something over 72,000, had jumped to over 350,000 in 1890.

The Catholicism of the immigrant waves as opposed to the older native Catholicism of Maryland or Louisiana, where a sort of modus vivendi had been established between Protestants and Catholics, took on something of the character of an alien religious colonization. It found its chief support in the foreign population herded in the great cities or the manufacturing centers. The immigrant who had lost touch with the traditions of the mother country still clung to his religion and brought with him his priest and a cultus which in form and spirit was essentially un-American. The situation was not helped by the fact that the Catholic Church is oriented in all matters of policy, whether religious, political, educational, or social, from a center outside the bounds of American society, namely, the Pope and his entourage at Rome. It was natural, furthermore, for Catholic leaders to make the unprecedented expansion of their church in America the basis for expressions of religious ambitions, not to say downright boastings, which contemplated nothing short of a Catholic America. Even as tactful a prelate as Cardinal Gibbons seems to have been tinged with this Catholic imperialism when in an enumeration of the contributions of his church to national life he said: "The birth rate in the United States is all in favor of the Church. The Irish, the Catholic Germans and Canadians are proverbially prolific; and there are other reasons which we may not enter upon here, and which point to an entirely disproportionate increase of Catholics in the near future." (*A Retrospect of Fifty Years*, Vol. I, p. 250.)

The high tide of Catholic imperialism in this country seems to have been reached in 1892 when Monsignor Satolli was sent as the Apostolic Delegate of the Vatican to the United States. Imperialistic ambitions cropped out in his address to the students of Gonzaga College in 1893 when he said, "The action of the Catholic faith and morality is favorable in every way to the direction in which the Constitution turns. The more public opinion and the government favor the Catholic schools the more will the welfare of the commonwealth be advanced. The Catholic education is the surest safeguard of the permanence throughout the centuries of the Constitution and

the best guide of the Republic in civic progress.
From this source the Constitution will gather that
assimilation so necessary for the perfect organization of the great progressive body which is the
American Republic.'' Here in vague and guarded
language we have applied to the future of America the central idea of Catholicism, namely, the assumption of a politico-religious unity in which the
central and commanding place is held by the
ecclesiastical super-nationalism of the Roman
Catholic Church.

These veiled indications of Catholic hopes of
transforming America into a Catholic nation
aroused wide-spread opposition, not only among
Protestants but even among patriotic Catholics.
The situation did not meet with the approval of
the majority of the American Catholic bishops.
Bishop Spalding, one of the most intelligent and
able of them, asserted, ''That the Delegate Satolli
has been and is a source of strength to the Apaists
(American Protective Association) there can be
no doubt. With us as in the Protestant world
generally, anti-Catholic prejudice is largely anti-
papal prejudice; and when the organs of public
opinion were filled with the sayings and doings of
'the American Pope' who though a foreigner, with
no intentions of becoming a citizen, ignorant alike

of our language and traditions, was supposed to have supreme authority in the Church in America, fresh fuel was thrown upon the fire of bigotry. The fact that his authority is ecclesiastical merely and concerns Catholics not as citizens but as members of the Church is lost sight of by the multitudes who are persuaded that the papacy is a political power eager to extend its control wherever opportunity may offer.''

The rapid growth of the Catholic Church called out the most rabid anti-Catholic movement in American history, namely, the American Protective Association. This A. P. A. Movement revived and strengthened the old traditional Protestant antipathy to Catholicism by identifying the Catholic Church with the alien and un-American elements introduced by immigration. These traditions of anti-Catholicism persisted after Apaism had died down as a political movement; they only needed some social strain or profound upheaval to bring them to the surface again. The war and the fears it kindled, especially the wide-spread distrust of all things foreign, naturally crystallized around this old traditional fear of the Catholic Church. In parts of the Middle West, where the American Protective Association found its main support, the Klan organizers have been endorsed by former members of the A. P. A., thus indicating the kinship of the two movements. One who takes the trouble to plot the area of the country, especially in the Middle West where the A. P. A. was strongest, will find that these sections have provided the Klan with its largest following.

The mantle of the American Protective Association, therefore, has fallen upon the shoulders of the Klan so far as anti-Catholicism is concerned. To-day, in communities where the Klan is rife, we meet with the same sensational stories circulated in the nineties, for example that the Catholics are storing arms in the basements of their churches and drilling at night. In Klan-ridden communities, as in Oregon, we find the familiar figure of the apostate monk or nun, more recent reproductions of the famous Maria Monk of A. P. A. days, touring the country at the instance of the Klan and revealing the secret machinations of the Catholic Church. And to-day, just as a generation ago, we find thousands of educated Americans lending an ear to these preposterous tales. To-day, just as in the early nineties, we find the Klan making use of anti-Catholic literature which, as in the case of the famous oath of the Knights of Columbus, has been proven to contain malicious and incredible slanders of fellow

Americans of the Catholic faith. In some sections of the country the Klan promoters have apparently resurrected old A. P. A. anti-Catholic literature.

In the case of the A. P. A. as of the Klan we meet with the same fundamental inconsistency between its platform of alleged principles and its actual conduct. The A. P. A. asserted, ''We attack no man's religion so long as he does not attempt to make his religion an element of political power.'' Yet a member of the A. P. A. was bound by his oath never to favor the nomination of a Catholic for public office nor to employ a Catholic in any services where a Protestant could be obtained. Similarly the Klan, as we have seen, insists, in the published statements of its ideals, upon complete religious toleration while in actual practice it encourages boycotts of Catholic and Jew in business and social relations. The A. P. A. movement boasted a system of espionage by which spies were detailed to report the doings of prominent Catholics and to make public the secret plottings of these enemies of the republic. Similarly the Klan boasts of a secret system of obtaining knowledge by which the Invisible Empire is able to ''see all and hear all.'' The member of the A. P. A., just as the modern Klansman, justified his secret

methods on the ground that in fighting the devil
you must make use of the devil's methods.

Three factors have combined to create in the
mind of the Klansman the feeling of a fundamental
incompatibility between the Catholic Church and
one hundred percent Americanism. The first of
these is the historic antagonism of Protestantism
to Catholicism. Where rock-ribbed evangelical
orthodoxy has persisted in most undiluted form,
as in the South, this antagonism has likewise persisted in the most pronounced fashion because sin-
cere but unenlightened religious loyalties have
acted as a preservative to perpetuate it. Powerful
sentiments, such as those aroused by religion, act
like a preserving medium upon ideas which they
happen to contain. These ideas, though often
false, persist because they are not subjected to
intelligent and effective criticism. They enjoy a
protected and hence artificial life, like that of
hot-house plants, which gives them the appearance
of being sacred and eternal verities. *Eterna non
caduca* is the favorite claim of the orthodox theolo-
gian for his creed, as opposed to the shifting
beliefs of the heretic. Thus do obsolete ideas,
especially in religion, maintain their form just
as the mummy of a Rameses, thanks to the skill
of the Egyptian embalmer, retains the actual fea-

tures of the ruler who has been dead some thirty-two hundred years.

This explains, in part at least, the paradoxical fact that anti-Catholicism is strongest in sections of the country such as Georgia, Texas or Oregon where the Catholics compose only a small fraction of the total population but where orthodox Protestantism reigns supreme. It is no accident that in those sections where the rigid frame-work of traditional orthodox Protestantism has been broken down, as in the larger centers of population, we find the most tolerant attitude among Protestants towards the members of the Catholic communion. This original antipathy of Protestantism to Catholicism was strengthened by a second factor, namely, that for the best part of a century a stream of aliens has flooded our shores, in the main members of the Catholic Church, thus serving to identify the Catholic Church in the mind of the native American with the alien and un-American forces in this country. Finally the political philosophy implicit in the super-nationalism of the Roman Catholic Church, like a Banquo's ghost that will not down, is ever arising to trouble the fancy of one hundred percent Americans made uneasy by situations involving the integrity of the nation's life.

III

There can be no intelligent criticism of the Klansman's condemnation of the Catholic Church as un-American without some knowledge of the development of the Catholic Church in America and the way in which American Catholics have reconciled loyalty to their country with loyalty to their church. At the beginning of our national life the Catholics were a negligible element. At the outbreak of the War of Independence they numbered hardly more than thirty thousand among a total population of three or four millions. This weak and despised minority stood up strongly for independence and religious toleration and furnished four signers of the Declaration of Independence, namely, Thomas Fitzsimmons, Thomas Sims Lee, and David and Charles Carroll.[1]

Though nominally enjoying the benefits of religious liberty, the Catholics for a generation or

[1] Under the leadership of John Carroll, made Bishop of Baltimore in 1790, the Catholics played such a noteworthy rôle in the struggle for freedom as to win the commendation of Washington. Washington's friendly and tolerant attitude may have given rise to the belief that he was a Catholic. The Catholic historian, Thomas O'Gorman, in his *History of the Roman Catholic Church in America*, p. 289, makes this curious statement, "Of late years some Catholic writers have claimed that Washington died a Catholic. At most we may perhaps say that he was thinking of such a step."

more after the revolution were ostracized by a
people who with their ministry held all Catholics
under suspicion. Two events did much, later on,
to break down this social isolation of the Catholics,
the onset of the Irish-Catholic immigration in the
thirties and the decay of Protestant orthodoxy
about the middle of the century. Describing the
status of the Catholics during the early decades
of the last century, DeTocqueville remarks: "If,
then, the Catholic citizens of the United States
are not forcibly led by the nature of their tenets
to adopt democratic and republican principles, at
least they are not necessarily opposed to them;
and their social position, as well as their limited
number, obliges them to adopt these opinions.
Most of the Catholics are poor, and they have no
chance of taking a part in the government unless
it be open to all the citizens. They constitute a
minority and all rights must be respected in order
to assure to them the free exercise of their own
privileges. These two causes induce them uncon-
sciously to adopt political principles which they
would perhaps support with less zeal if they were
rich and preponderant. The Catholic clergy of
the United States has never attempted to oppose
this political tendency but seeks rather to justify
its results. The priests of America have divided

the intellectual world into two parts; in the one
they place the doctrines of revealed religion, which
command their assent; in the other they leave
those truths which they believe to have been freely
left open to the researches of political inquiry.
Thus the Catholics of the United States are at
the same time the most faithful believers and the
most zealous citizens'' (*Democracy in America,*
Colonial Press, ed. I, p. 306).

It will be seen at once that the situation of the
Catholic Church in America, characterized with
keen insight by DeTocqueville, is full of interesting possibilities. In the first place, here is a great
historic faith which has always insisted upon the
union of church and state, forced to develop under
political institutions requiring the separation of
church and state. Moreover, the exigencies of the
situation, namely, the poverty and numerical
weakness of the Catholics, made it to their advantage to insist upon this very separation of church
and state in spite of the fact that it is antagonistic to the traditional Catholic point of view.
For, obviously, any intervention by a state, predominantly Protestant in its sympathies, in the
affairs of Catholics would be unwelcome. To exist
at all, the Catholic Church was forced at the out-
set to take a position hardly in harmony with its

traditions. Under the Constitution it must be content to be merely one of many rival religious faiths, all tolerated alike, all enjoying equal rights before the law. The Catholic Church, through the sheer force of circumstances, its own traditional dogmas to the contrary notwithstanding, was thus compelled to acknowledge in actual practice, if not in theory, that its claim to be the only true and authoritative religion had no greater validity in the eyes of the state than other similar claims by rival faiths. Such a situation tended to create in the thought and life of American Catholics a curious dualism which historic Catholicism has never tolerated. It is the dualism created by the enforced separation of secular and religious matters. This gives rise to two sets of loyalties constantly bidding for the control of American Catholics. On the one hand, we have the intimate spiritual and institutional life of the Church with its international ramifications; on the other, the practical civic and social life of American Catholics as members of American society. Which is to take precedence?

It is interesting to surmise what would have been the future of American Catholicism had it been free to develop, as did the other religious faiths of America, through the normal increase of the Catholic population. It is quite possible that we should have seen in time the emergence in this country of a phase of Catholicism that would have modified profoundly the Catholic Church as a whole. But the forces at work, which if left free might have given us a thoroughly Americanized Catholicism, were constantly being offset by the immigrant tide from Europe. This vast stream of European Catholicism made difficult the development of a purely American type of Catholicism and assured in the end the preservation of the identity of European and American Catholicism. The leaders of American Catholicism, especially at first, were recruited from Europe, being French, German, or Irish by birth. Even in the case of native-born Americans, their training was gotten in the Catholic institutions of Europe and not in America. The early immigrants, especially the Irish, were soldiers of fortune, and exhausted their resources in reaching this country. Hence they settled as laborers in the large cities of the East. American Catholicism has always been mainly urban. This made it an easy matter to organize parishes and place over them priests trained in Europe. The priests of later Catholic immigrants often spoke only the language of their people. To these factors tending to preserve the traditions of European Catholicism must be added the ever-watchful eye of Rome, jealous for the purity of the Catholic faith and the supremacy of the Apostolic See.

Catholicism, therefore, remained until well towards the middle of the century more or less an alien and exotic growth in American life. The flood of immigrants of the Catholic faith was mainly responsible for this. They kept the majority of the membership of the church alien in complexion. They effectually prevented the development of a type of Catholicism that could be called American. They gave to the Know-Nothings and even to the Apaists an excuse for charging the Catholic Church with being alien and un-American. It was not until the third quarter of the century that a movement began to take shape within the Catholic Church giving some idea of what a purely American type of Catholicism might be. "Americanism" is the general name for this movement, though the term seems to have been used for the first time in 1884 in connection with the language controversy in the Catholic schools. It has now come to be synonymous with the nationalist and liberal movement within American Catholicism. (See Albert Houtin, *L'Américanisme,* Paris, 1904.)

In 1893 Archbishop Ireland of St. Paul wrote, "The American current which for a quarter of a century runs so plainly in the ocean of Catholicism, goes back, as it seems to me, in large measure to Father Hecker and his early collaboration." (*Introduction to the Life of Father Hecker*.) Isaac Thomas Hecker was born in New York in 1819 and inherited something of a mystical and ascetic temperament from his mother who was a devout Methodist. He took orders in the Catholic Church, was dismissed from the Redemptorist order of which he was a member and straightway founded the order of the Paulists of which he was the superior, and in 1865 established the *Catholic World*. The chief object of his order was the commendation of the Catholic faith to the non-Catholic world. He approached his task from the point of view of a native-born American with a minimum of interest in medieval theology, ancient religious forms, and the passive virtues of the religious recluse. He sought to bring the Catholic faith into thorough harmony with American life. The fundamental notes of his preachings were social and democratic.

The disciples of Hecker were never numerous; at the turn of the century the Paulists numbered hardly more than a dozen. But their influence was far and away out of proportion to their numbers. For they were consecrated to the imperative task of overcoming the national prejudice against the Catholic Church. They sought to remove the barriers that were preventing the Catholics from becoming an integral part of the American nation. The success they attained inspired many of the Catholic clergy, not members of the Paulist order. To be sure, the reactionaries dubbed them the "Catholic Yankees," but by the end of the third quarter of the century, thanks largely to the influence of Hecker's followers, Catholicism in this country began to assume a distinctly American air. Either directly connected with the movement set going by Hecker or sympathetic with it were the most distinguished prelates of American Catholicism. Cardinal Gibbons, the greatest of native-born American Catholics, paid him high tribute. Archbishop Ireland, perhaps the most intensely American member of this group, acknowledges the inspiration he gained from Father Hecker. Archbishop Keane, the first head of the Catholic University at Washington, was a novice of the Paulists. Thomas O'Gorman, Professor in the Catholic University, was a member of this society. The able Archbishop of Peoria, John

Lancaster Spalding, was an intimate friend of the Paulists.

The Catholic Church and the American people owe an incalculable debt to these able and patriotic leaders of the American movement. With tact and courage they guided their people through the storm and stress of Apaism. By their acts as well as by their public utterances they did much to convince the mass of non-Catholic Americans that loyalty to the Catholic Church and loyalty to the American flag are not incompatible terms. Their Americanism was above reproach. The ignorant and bigoted Klan leaders, as well as many intolerant Protestant pastors, would do well to familiarize themselves with the utterances of these Catholic leaders. Cardinal Gibbons, on the occasion of his acceptance of the Cardinal's hat at Rome in 1887, remarked, "I say with a feeling of profound pride and gratitude that I belong to a country where the civil government extends over us the ægis of its protection without interfering with the legitimate exercise of our mission as ministers of the Gospel of Christ." This same Catholic leader closes his noteworthy address, "The Church and the Republic," with these words, "American Catholics rejoice in our sepa-

ration of church and state; and I can conceive of
no combination of circumstances likely to arise
which would make a union desirable either to
church or state."

Bishop Spalding, in answer to the charge of the
Apaists that the Catholics are the foes of the
public schools, says: "In a country such as ours
no other system of state schools seems to be possible and we are openly and without reserve in
favor of free schools, and, consequently, in favor
of a school tax. For my part—and I think I express the Catholic view—I not only would not,
had I the power, destroy the public school system,
but would leave nothing undone to develop and
perfect it" ("Catholicism and Apaism," *North
American Review*, Vol. 159, p. 286). Archbishop
Ireland in an eloquent address delivered in 1895
said: "Let me say this to Catholic Americans: Be
Americans in the best and truest sense of the word
American. Love America, love her institutions;
be devoted to her interests, quick to defend her,
slow to criticize her. In the past the Church in
America, due to the necessity of circumstances,
was alien in appearance and accent. It would be
ridiculous to say that she did not suffer from it.
In order to remove or to forestall every mistake,
every suspicion, we must for the love of church

and country almost exaggerate in our hearts and emphasize in our lives our Americanism. We must not make a gesture nor pronounce a word which can be made a pretext for the belief that we are not in intimate accord with our country." (Re-translated from the French of Houtin, *op. cit.*, p. 163.)

The liberal and nationalist movement within the Catholic Church met with determined opposition which emerged in most pronounced fashion, perhaps, in connection with the language question in the Catholic schools in the late eighties. The Catholic clergy, in their desire to maintain a censorship upon the thinking of the faithful, have as a rule favored small and local language groups rather than the universal languages in which are written the great masterpieces, often dangerous to orthodox faith. For this reason apparently the French priests have sought to retain local languages such as the Basque, the Breton, the Flemish, and the Alsatian patois. So long as the teaching is done in these languages the pupils remain safe from the poison of a Renan or a Voltaire. Many of the Catholic clergy of America seemed inclined at first to follow a similar policy with the immigrant groups under their charge. They remarked that the immigrants who learned English were in danger of becoming Protestants or of falling into religious indifference or unbelief. They insisted, therefore, that the children of the immigrants should be taught in the language of their parents. The German Catholics took the lead in this sectarian and un-American attitude on the language issue. They were opposed by the Irish Catholics who were zealous for speedy Americanization. The Irish accused the Germans of lack of loyalty towards their new fatherland. The Germans replied by accusing the Irish of "Americanism," which now came to be a comprehensive term by which the reactionary Catholic group characterized the new liberal and nationalist movement.

The language controversy became so serious that it attracted the attention of the Vatican and added a new word to the language, "Cahenslyism," which Webster's *International* defines as "A plan proposed to the Pope in 1891 by P. P. Cahensly, a member of the German parliament, to divide the foreign-born population of the United States, for ecclesiastical purposes, according to European nationalities, and to appoint bishops and priests of like race and speaking the same language as the majority of the members of a diocese or congregation." Under the leadership of Bishop Keane and other "Americanists" this move was defeated.

The national and liberal movement in American Catholicism, which triumphed in the language controversy, was responsible for the creation of a Catholic university at Washington, the foundation stone of which was laid in 1888 in the presence of Cardinal Gibbons and the president of the republic, Bishop Spalding delivering the chief address. Americanism reached something like a culmination in the part played by Catholics in the Chicago Exposition and the Parliament of Religions in 1893. Under liberal leadership the Catholics were winning the respect and confidence of all intelligent Americans and that in spite of the bitter opposition of Apaism.

Just when liberal Catholic Americanism seemed to have won for itself a clear field in this country it was tottering to its fall. The liberal movement had considered itself fortunate in that it arose under the rule of the cultured and tactful Pope Leo XIII whom American Catholics praised as the Pope designed by Providence to reconcile the modern world to Catholicism. It appears, however, that even Pope Leo XIII began in time to fear and distrust Americanism. His official historian wrote in 1894, "It cannot be denied that great dangers menace the Church in the United States because of the spirit of independence innate in the soul of every American." The quarrel between the liberal and reactionary parties crept into the Catholic University at Washington with most unfortunate results. The liberals were led by the rector, Keane, the reactionaries by the two professors of German extraction, Schroeder and Pohle, the former becoming the real leader of the Cahensly party. The Irish-American element in the university made the atmosphere very uncomfortable for Schroeder. Finally in September, 1896, Leo XIII notified Rector Keane that he was deposed. This exhibition of autocratic power over the life and thought of American citizens by a foreigner created a profound stir in the intellectual life not only of the Catholic Church but of the nation. A meeting was held in Carroll Institute, Washington, in which men and women of all faiths joined to express their respect for the deposed rector. At this meeting a speaker declared, "It is Bishop Rector Keane who first made me understand what is an American Catholic. All my life I have heard the Roman Catholic described as a man imbued in the matter of personal and national liberty with ideas that are strange and medieval. . . . But here is a man endowed with the veritable American spirit. This in his invincible logic: our institutions are free institutions; they must dominate the world; they are impossible without liberty of speech and liberty in the schools. Therefore we must have free speech and free schools."

The attitude of the Catholic liberals towards this move of Leo XIII is exceedingly suggestive. Bishop Keane read publicly the pontifical letter removing him from office and his own reply, adding these words, "I do not ask reasons; I beg you, my friends, and you, students, do as I have done. Do not ask why the Holy Father has done this. It is sufficient that he has done it for it to have been done wisely and well." The prelate then withdrew to a sanatorium in California, presumably to rest his shattered nerves. A year later in a sermon in Washington, Archbishop Ireland made use of this language: "Those who are stubborn and rebellious against Leo XIII are to be found outside of France. They are to be found where they are least to be expected—in America. There are naturally divisions among the Catholics of America, not in regard to truth in matters of faith and morals but in the tendencies and movements and in the adjustments to modern circumstances and environment. There should be for us but one tendency, one movement, one method of adjustment, those indicated by Leo. Separation from Leo, opposition to his directions, is nothing else than rebellion no matter what the efforts to dissimulate in America, as in France, under the specious names of conservatism, traditional Catholicism, religious fear of innovations. Those who resist in America the direction indicated by Leo are rebels though they claim to be the only true and loyal Catholics. The loyal Catholics have but one name, Catholics. They have but one rule of action, the will and the example of Leo. . . . When I withdraw from Catholics it is because they are stubborn. When the French Catholics are with the Pope I am with the French Catholics; when they are against him I am against them. When the German Catholics are with the Pope, I am with them; when they are against the Pope, I am against them.'' (Re-translated from the French of Albert Houtin, *L'Américanisme*, p. 153.) Thus was the issue joined between the Pope and the nationalistic and liberal element in American Catholicism, and—Rome won.

IV

In the light of this sketch of American Catholicism what shall we say of the aspersions made by the Klan against its fellow citizens of the Catholic faith? In the first place, it must be said that the Klan shows gross and unpardonable ignorance of the actual facts of the history of American Catholicism. It is unaware that within the circle of the Catholic Church the problem of Americanism has been fought out, especially in connection with the language question, and that American Catholics have proven their Americanism by their deeds. In the second place, the Klan and its abettors have been cruelly and stupidly unjust towards their fellow citizens of the Catholic faith in that they hold them personally responsible for the persecutions and misdeeds of the past. It is just as logical to blame the descendants of the Puritans for witch-burning as to blame Catholics of to-day for the Spanish Inquisition. Cardinal Gibbons has repudiated in public print the crimes of the Inquisition; they cannot be laid at the door of American Catholicism. Again, the Klan and its supporters have laid themselves open to the charge that in spite of their boasted championship of American liberties,

American Catholics and not the Klan are the real
supporters of religious freedom. So far as the
surface facts of this unfortunate situation are
concerned, many Catholics have far greater right
to be called one hundred percent American than
the leaders of the Klan. Finally, there is no more
preposterous assumption than that put forward
by Klan leaders to the effect that the Catholic
Church is a menace to the sovereignty of the
American nation. "Our obedience to the Pope,"
says Bishop Spalding, "is confined to the domain
of religious faith, morals, and discipline; and
since the state, with us at least, claims no jurisdiction over such matters, there can be no question
of conflict. We have, and none are more thankful
for it than the Catholics, a separation of the
church from the state. . . . The Pope has never
attempted to interfere in the civil or political affairs of this country, and were he to attempt to
do so his action would be resented by the Catholics more quickly than by others" (*North American Review,* Vol. 159, p. 284).

To bear witness to the unimpeachable patriotism of American Catholics, however, and to condemn the stupid bigotry of the Klan does not ex-
haust the situation. It does not explain, for example, why for the best part of a hundred years

these anti-Catholic movements have arisen to trouble American life. It does not explain why thousands of intelligent Americans who repudiate the brutal intolerance of the Klan sympathize in their hearts with its anti-Catholicism. It does not explain why similar anti-Catholic movements have arisen in other countries such as "anti-clericalisme" in France and the famous *Kultur-kampf* of the days of Bismarck in Germany.

Rev. W. R. Inge, Dean of St. Paul's, London, who can hardly be accused of affiliations with the Ku Klux Klan, makes the following animadversions upon European Catholicism: "On the whole it can hardly be denied that it has been a failure. It does not seem to have raised the moral tone of society in the countries which have adopted it, except perhaps in such Arcadian communities as Oberammergau and in some very limited circles living an old-fashioned life under priestly direction. It has shown all the defects of despotism— a costly and luxurious central government, necessitating heavy taxation and the ruthless suppression of all movements towards freedom. This kind of oppression is peculiarly searching and tyrannical under a theocracy because it lays its hands not only on overt acts, but upon all liberty of thought. To think for one's self in matters

which concern our eternal interest is rebellion or
treason. The faithful are forbidden to read certain books and to join certain societies; they
must submit their consciences to periodical ex-
amination by an official; the education of their
children is taken out of their hands and is strictly
regulated by the hierarchy. An acute conflict of
loyalties is set up between Church and State; no
Catholic is more than conditionally a patriot, and
the conditions are of the political and not of the
moral order. . . . Conscience is stifled; and the
Catholic is curiously impervious to that lay morality which with all its defects generally embodies
the best features of a national character. These
defects are, of course, not in any way connected
with the Christian religion; *they are the defects
of theocratic autocracy in its Catholic form. . . .*[1]
This experiment is not played out; it may even
have a great future if, as is probable, the present
riot of nationalism is followed by a struggle between two or more types of internationalism.
But it has certainly not solved the problem of human government." (*Outspoken Essays,* second
series, p. 111.)

I am not concerned here to pronounce upon the
justice of these strictures of "the gloomy dean"

[1] The italics are the author's.

upon the Catholic Church. They hardly apply,
without some modifications, to American Catholicism. What is important for present purposes is the dean's assertion that the genius of
the Catholic Church centers around the fact that
it is a "theocratic autocracy." The dramatic surrender of the leaders of liberal American Catholicism to the will of Pope Leo XIII when he removed
Bishop Keane from the rectorship of the Catholic
University and Archbishop Ireland's eloquent
glorification of "the will of Leo" indicate beyond
a doubt that American Catholicism is likewise a
"theocratic autocracy." That is to say, the supreme law of this vast super-national organization is vested in the will of the Pope as the vicegerent of God on earth. The one doctrine which
Father Hecker and his followers of the Catholic
liberal party seemed inclined to stress was that
of Papal infallibility. It follows, therefore, that
in any discussion of the troublous question of
Catholicism and nationalism we must start with
this fact of the theocratic and autocratic nature
of the Catholic Church. It will be found to throw
much light upon the attitudes of devout Catholics
upon all matters, national, educational, social,
moral, as well as religious.

About a year after the close of the war the

Catholic hierarchy of America met as a body at the Catholic University in Washington and issued a pastoral letter. Touching in that letter upon the perturbed post-war conditions this statement was made: "It is imperative that we recognize in God the source of justice and right; in his law the sovereign rule of life; in the destiny he has appointed for us the ultimate standard by which all values are fixed and determined." Without entering into the difficult questions as to what God's law is, how we are to give it practical formulation, and how we are to base upon it the vast and complex machinery of civil law, we have here obviously a formulation of the Catholic social ideal in theocratic terms. On the surface, this theocratic statement of the social ideal tallies with that of orthodox Protestantism which finds in God's revealed will the source of all law and justice. There is, however, this fundamental difference. Since the breakdown of the Calvinistic theocracies of Geneva and New England the social ideal of Protestantism has always remained more of a "counsel of perfection" than a concrete social program. The strict separation of church and state in America has forced Protestantism to assume an inspirational rather than a practical rôle. The influence of the Church is moral and spiritual, rather than practical or political. The result of all this is that the ethics of politics, business, education, or science has become thoroughly secularized. That is to say, we have built up within these various groups a body of ethical norms which, while not necessarily antagonistic to, are at least non-committal on religion. This does not mean to say that teacher, business man, politician, or scientist may not be deeply religious. But so far as the ethical sanctions that govern these various occupations are concerned, they are primarily secular rather than religious in nature.

The essentially theocratic nature of the Roman Catholic Church does not permit this separation of the secular and the religious. The formulation of the social ideal can never be for the Catholic a mere "counsel of perfection." To exist at all it must find some concrete institutional form. A religious ideal of society that is not actually incarnated in institutions, or does not imply as its correlative possible institutional formulation, is from the Catholic point of view unthinkable and non-existent. Here, then, we have a fundamental difference between the genius of Catholicism which is essentially Latin and the genius of Protestantism which is subjective, spiritual, and individualistic, or if you please, Anglo-Saxon. For historical Protestantism "the kingdom of God is within you" and its external manifestations are more or less accidental. The mental attitude is the important thing. For the Catholic the kingdom of God is both within you and without you but the latter or the institutional formulation is the important thing. Inner attitudes are created, safeguarded, made practical by fixed external regulations in sacraments, cultus, educational system, or ecclesiastical polity.

It is possible to liken the historic Catholic Church to the Gothic cathedral, the most beautiful artistic product of the Catholic faith. The essence of the Gothic as opposed to the Romanesque structure is its principle of balanced thrusts. Around this great architectonic principle are arranged flying buttresses, pointed arches, fluted pillars, stained glass windows, and soaring nave. While this basic architectural principle remains fixed there is often the greatest variety and plasticity in the arrangement of details. Contrast, for example, the Doric simplicity of Notre Dame de Paris with the flamboyant richness of the cathedral of Rheims, now, alas, a ruin! Like the Gothic cathedral the Catholic Church has one great architectonic principle, its theocratic structure, of which the doctrine of papal infallibility is merely the logical expression. The secret of the marvellous success with which this church has adapted herself to diverse climes and civilizations is to be found in her ability to permit the greatest freedom and variety in matters of detail while maintaining her essentially theocratic structure. Witness the skill with which she has adapted herself to the free institutions of this country without sacrificing her basic principle or even suggesting that it is incompatible with the genius of democracy. It is only when she fears this basic principle is endangered, as apparently in the case of Bishop Keane and the Catholic liberals, that she reluctantly reveals her essentially autocratic nature.

v

What are some of the practical implications of the foregoing remarks for the problem of Catholicism and Americanism? They imply, first, that every Catholic who is at the same time a patriotic American and a devout subject of the Pope must be an opportunist on the question of the separation of church and state. That is to say, the patriotic Catholic, viewing the unprecedented prosperity of his church in this country under a régime of separation of church and state and realizing that this

separation is directly responsible for this prosperity and realizing furthermore that anything
else is impossible, accepts the situation gladly and
proclaims his hearty assent to this fundamental
principle of Americanism. At the same time, if
he reflects upon the genius of his church, he must
realize that the theocratic social ideal which the
papacy has never relinquished presupposes the
union of church and state. Thus Cardinal Gibbons, who closed his address, ''The Church and
the Republic,'' with the statement, ''American
Catholics rejoice in our separation of church and
state,'' in which statement he is undoubtedly sin-
cere, likewise said in this same address that a
union of church and state is ''ideally best.'' Such
union is ''ideally best'' in that it carries out the
logic of the essentially theocratic structure of the
Catholic Church and best realizes its social ideal.

Again in the matter of religious liberty and toleration the devout Catholic pursues an opportu-
nistic policy. The Klansman has foolishly allowed
himself to be jockeyed into the position in which
he is, in actual fact, the opponent of tolerance
while his Catholic adversary is really its champion. It is the logic of circumstances, however,
rather than devotion to the principle of toleration
that determines the Catholic attitude. The de-

vout Catholic for whom the immediate practical problem is his status in American democracy has no other choice than to champion religious toleration. For he is well aware that the principle of religious toleration has been of incalculable value to him in finding a foothold in a country essentially Protestant and traditionally prejudiced against all things Catholic. The principle of toleration, however, is hardly compatible with a theocratic autocracy. Catholicism has only admitted tolerance as a matter of expediency, never as a moral principle of the intellectual and spiritual life. In his encyclical of November 1, 1885, Leo XIII states, "Although the Church does not concede that every kind of divine worship is lawful by the same right as the true religion, nevertheless she does not condemn those rulers of commonwealths who, for the sake of some great good to be gained or evil to be avoided, permit, in toleration, according to the manners and usages of the country, each kind of religious profession to have its place."

A Catholic writer has interpreted the Pope's encyclical to mean that the Catholic Church can never admit "that every religion has intrinsically equal rights" for the simple reason that her faith is true while other faiths are false. It follows, therefore, that for tolerance in the sense of "a system that dispenses the same level measure of commendation to all religions, a doctrine that proclaims all religious professions of equal worth and equal right before God and as far as salvation is concerned, the Church has nothing but reprobation." (Rev. T. Brosnahan, S. J., *Donahoe's Magazine,* Jan. 1894). Such a position, patently at variance with the traditional American conception of tolerance, is obviously the logical result of the dominant idea of theocratic absolutism. For granting that there is but one true Church of which the Pope is the head, that this church is the sole depository of divine saving truth, it follows that it is the duty of this church to proclaim herself as the infallible guide of sinful men and to warn against other false faiths. Tolerance then becomes a sin. It is not supposed for once that the average American of Catholic persuasion acts upon such a doctrine. It remains in abeyance just as do similar "hard" doctrines of orthodox Protestantism. Patriotic American Catholics are too thoroughly convinced of the practical value of tolerance for their own church ever to challenge it.

Now when we throw together in a free democratic society two types of religion, one of which accepts religious tolerance as a vital principle of society, the other as a mere matter of expediency and hence to be repudiated when circumstances require it, we get a very interesting situation. Tolerance for Baptist, Methodist, or Presbyterian means a fair field and the right to compete with other sects for the religious loyalties of men. Tolerance for the Catholic Church, not necessarily intentionally but in actual practice, means merely license for carrying out the logic of a theocratic autocracy. Protestantism thus finds itself in competition with a church which does not accept the rule of a fair field except as a matter of expediency, that does not treat the various forms of Protestantism as legitimate rivals but as erroneous and dangerous deviations from the true faith and therefore to be eradicated. The situation is of course intensified by the fact that Protestantism is nationalistic, divided, and unorganized while the Catholic Church is essentially a militant international organization and enabled by virtue of a vast hierarchy utterly loyal to the Pope to pursue its aims independent of national conditions and thus to utilize all its forces in the most effective fashion. Under these circumstances Protestant antipathy to Catholicism does not seem wholly without justification. These facts must be honestly faced before we condemn offhand the anti-Catholicism of the Klan.

It would be a mistake, however, to conclude from the foregoing remarks that there is no place in the theocratic ideal of Catholicism for liberty. Cardinal Gibbons, whose patriotism and intellectual honesty will hardly be challenged, claims that the papacy is the mightiest ally of freedom. In the past, he asserts, "The popes were on the side of liberty and the people, against the despotism of the crown. The papacy was then universally considered the embodiment of justice and liberty upon earth." It follows, therefore, that "in an age of democracy and liberty some gratitude might be expected for the most powerful defender of the people and of liberty; yet the very success of the papacy in their defence is the ground of the prejudice that exists against it" (*op. cit.* p. 226). Such language is highly enigmatical until we make clear the notion of liberty it presupposes. The idea of liberty has two phases. Considered from the institutional point of view a nation is free when it is provided with the wisest and best laws for the fullest possible development of its citizens. Considered from the individual point of view a nation is free when it offers the largest opportunity for the creative and untrammelled self-expression of its citizens. The two ideas seem contradictory. For how can there be free, creative self-expression where one is hedged about by law and authority? On the other hand, how can we talk intelligibly about self-expression except as it finds rational and effective direction through the aid of law and authority? If we stress the one phase we get anarchy; if we stress the other we get despotism. We need the element of law and order without which there is no stability; we need also the element of free, untrammelled self-expression without which there is no progress. The problem of civilization and government is to preserve the happy balance between these two phases of liberty.

Cardinal Gibbons, in his references to the contributions of his church to liberty, evidently has in mind the institutional and authoritarian phase of liberty. If we assume, as does the devout Catholic, the theocratic autocracy of the Catholic Church, with its closed system of doctrines, laws, and ordinances embracing every phase of life and providing a final solution for all human problems, its infallible interpreter of the meaning and application of those doctrines in the Pope, God's vicegerent on earth, its vast politico-

religious supernationalism knit into one effective
organic whole by a hierarchy absolutely loyal to
the Pope, its educational system devised to meet
the needs of this supernationalism rather than the
needs of the citizens of any one nation and
planned so to shape the thoughts and acts of the
individual from the cradle as to make him a happy
and loyal citizen of this supernation—if we are
willing to grant these assumptions, then the language of Cardinal Gibbons, paradoxical and even
impertinent as it may sound to the Klansman, is
perfectly intelligible and justifiable.

VI

In the light of the foregoing discussion it is perhaps possible now for us to state the permanent
issue that underlies the Klan's anti-Catholicism.
The Klan's attempt to impeach the patriotism of
the millions of Catholic Americans is absurd and
cruelly unjust. The Klan's claim that the Pope is
making use of the vast organization of which he
is the head to intermeddle in the political affairs
of this country is ridiculous and childish. The
occupants of the chair of Saint Peter have long
since given up any schemes of political imperialism. The Pope, however, has not relinquished his

claim to what may be called a moral and spiritual imperialism, that is to say, the sovereign right to settle, as the mouthpiece of the living God, all disputes of mankind at the higher level of their moral and religious loyalties. There should be, in theory at least, no conflict between the political sovereignty of America and the spiritual sovereignty claimed by the Pope over all Christendom and actually exercised over some twenty million Americans of Catholic faith. These two types of sovereignty, however, only avoid a clash in so far as the American state, on the one hand, assures to all Catholics complete freedom to worship God according to the dictates of their consciences and in so far as the theocratic absolutism of the papacy, on the other hand, restricts itself solely to the spiritual sphere.

The danger point in this adjustment of sovereignties lies in the fact, already pointed out, that the spiritual sovereignty of the papacy, thanks to its inherent logic and great historic traditions, is constantly seeking concrete institutional form. Considered from the point of view of the logic of a theocratic autocracy, the parochial school system is the natural and necessary instrument for assuring to the church a body of believers entirely in sympathy with this spiritual sovereignty of the

Pope. In the more or less hostile atmosphere of our modern industrial democracy the parochial school is about the only agency that can assure the continuance of that spiritual sovereignty over Americans. But the parochial school must also perform another task. It must train prospective American citizens so as to secure their loyal and intelligent acceptance of the political sovereignty of the state. The state permits the parochial schools only on this assumption. The parochial school system, therefore, attempts to train subjects for two types of sovereignties, one moral and religious, the other political and secular. It seeks to make men and women subject to the Pope in religious matters and subject to the state in political matters. It is the difficulty of blending these two sovereignties that makes the parochial school system such an anomaly in American society and such a bone of contention between the Nativists and the Catholics. The Catholic claims the right to educate his child in a church school on the ground that spiritual sovereignty lies outside the sphere of the state; the Nativist, as represented by the Klan, claims that a sovereign state should train its own future citizens. It is the presence of these two sovereignties and the charge that they necessitate more or less of a divided allegiance on the part of our Catholic citizenship that underlies all anti-Catholic movements, including that of the Klan. The charge of divided allegiance is doubtless unjust, though the Catholic Church emphatically discourages the critical independence of thought so necessary to citizenship in a democracy. The vast majority of good Catholics, to be sure, do not feel that their loyalty to the Pope decreases in the slightest their loyalty to a democratic state. But so long as even this semblance of a divided allegiance exists there will not be lacking one hundred percent Americans to make it the basis of an attack upon Catholicism. We have, therefore, to conclude this rather lengthy discussion with the somewhat discouraging remark of the historian quoted earlier in this chapter, "The time-honored Anglo-Saxon and Evangelical aspersion of the integrity of Catholic citizenship . . . though diminishing in force from generation to generation is, nevertheless, liable to recur in years to come" and especially "during future flurries of intolerance."

CHAPTER VII

SECRECY AND CITIZENSHIP

"No state of society or laws can render men so much alike," remarks DeTocqueville, "but that education, fortune, and tastes will interpose some differences between them. . . . They will, therefore, always tend to evade the provisions of legislation, whatever they may be; and departing in some respect from the circle within which they were to be bound, they will set up, close by the great political community, small private circles, united together by the similitude of their conditions, habits and manners." It would be expected, therefore, that secret fraternal societies would early make their appearance in American society as a natural means of escape from the standardizing effect of conventional democracy. Furthermore, it would seem that the fraternal society would be the natural protection of men against the dangerous isolation of the individual encouraged by the *laissez faire* democracy of the first part of the last century with its strenuous empha-

207

sis upon the principle of equality. It is rather surprising, therefore, to find that apart from some of the older secret societies, such as the Free Masons, few secret organizations arose in this country before the last quarter of the century. At the close of the century eighty-six percent of the fraternal orders were only twenty years old.

I

Certain conditions in American life at first discouraged the rise of the secret society. Foremost among these we must place the inherent antagonism of a highly individualistic pioneer democracy to secret societies as essentially undemocratic. There was also a lack, at first, of that measure of socialization and mutualization of human relations which the fraternal order seems to require. Finally, intense antagonism was aroused against all secret societies by an incident which happened in Batavia, New York, in 1826. One William Morgan incurred the hostility of the Masons by announcing the publication of a book revealing their secrets. He was abducted, presumably by the Masons, and all trace of him disappeared. The indignation aroused by the mysterious doom of Morgan became intense and took on political form. The Masons, it was claimed, placed their secret oath above their civic duties and were therefore dangerous to good government. An anti-Masonic state organization put candidates in the field in 1830. In 1832 the anti-Masons assumed the proportions of a national party, nominating William Wirt for the presidency. This antagonism to secret societies was inherited by the Whig party which elected Seward governor of New York state in 1838 and Harrison president in 1840.

When a large part of the Whig party was absorbed by the Republican party the anti-Masonic tradition was continued in such men as Thurlow Weed, Millard Fillmore, and W. H. Seward. The reforming moral idealism that lent such initial vitality to the Republican party and found its strongest expression in the Abolition movement, had as little place in its social ideal for secret societies as for the institution of slavery. Wendell Phillips, the orator and abolitionist, in a letter to Rev. J. P. Stoddard of Boston, March 18th, 1880, wrote: "A secret society is wholly out of place under democratic institutions. Every secret society, so far as it is wide-spread and influential, threatens the purity and essence of such institutions and warps them to private ends and class supremacy. Secret societies prevent the impartial execution of the laws and obstruct the necessary and wholesome action of political parties. The judge on the bench, the juryman in the box, and all the machinery of politics feel the tyranny of secret societies. No judge, and no executive officer, especially in a republic, can, with any self-respect, be a member of a secret society. He lays himself open to suspicion, subjects himself to dangerous temptation, and sets an evil example.''

The Protestant churches, especially that branch of Protestantism closely affiliated with the idealistic and reforming atmosphere of the Abolition movement, namely, Congregationalism, added its contribution to the opposition to secret societies. Deacon Philo Carpenter, a philanthropic Congregationalist of Chicago, ''having come out of the anti-Masonic turmoil of New York state, and being imbued with the reformatory spirit of that revival era,'' left a sum of money ''to be used in opposition to secret societies.'' This fund was offered in prizes for essays on the relation of secret societies to Christian citizenship and three of the best essays were published in 1897 under the title ''Secrecy and Citizenship.'' Their authors were Congregational ministers. The opposition of the church to secret societies as expressed in these essays is political, moral, and religious. It is argued that secret societies are inimical to free democratic institutions because "citizenship in a free state seeks the equal welfare of all the members of the same, the strong and the weak alike, the grown men, the women and the little children, the dependent and the fortunate, the able and the defective. . . . But an oath-bound, exclusive, secret society—whether a monastery, a convent, a lodge of Jesuits or of Free Masons, the Mafia, or the Clan-na-Gael, or whatsoever else refusing to permit the state, that is the whole people, to know its purposes and methods, closed in by hostile and repelling barriers, shutting out the state and its representatives as such—not only has no place as a friendly and essential body within the state, but is contrary to the purpose and character of all those other groups, which make up the essential parts of the state" (*Secrecy and Citizenship*, p. 20 f.).

It is argued, in the second place, that secret societies are immoral because "no man can bind himself by oath or pledge to keep secret what he does not yet know without thereby bartering away his moral freedom. This is the fundamental error in all the secret orders which vitiates everything in connection with them. . . . What the individual has thus pledged himself to keep secret may prove, when he comes to it, to be a legitimate object of secrecy, but he did not know this when he made his oath. If, on the contrary, the things which he learns, as he goes forward, prove to be iniquitous or for other reasons deserving publicity he finds himself bound, in the most emphatic way, by his own promise, not to divulge them. He must, therefore, either violate the plainest demands of his conscience and abide by his oath of secrecy or obey the present behests of duty, make known the things which he has learned, and thereby confess the sin committed in the beginning" (*op. cit.*, p. 54 f.). This situation "inevitably induces a degree of moral blindness and indifference to duty," and it "creates among the members of the orders a habit of concealment, an indirectness of speech amounting often to actual falsehood; the result is permanent impairment of the sense of truth and of truthful expression."

Finally, secret orders, it is alleged, are fundamentally un-Christian, for "the first element in a Christian life is personal loyalty to Jesus Christ as Saviour, Teacher, and Lord. Every form of oath-bound secrecy involves disloyalty to him in some of these aspects. One can not become a member of the simplest and relatively best of the secret societies without violating some of his teachings about light, openness of character, purity of association, avoidance of oaths, universal love and brotherhood'' (*op. cit.,* p. 68). The secret society is also inimical to orthodox faith. ''No religious tenets must be tolerated that would trouble the devotee of any religious system or even press upon the conscience of the irreligious too closely. The very nature of the secret growth, along the lines which it lays down, and of which it boasts, tends to narrow down all religious convictions to the vanishing point, that the most diverse elements religiously may be grouped as brothers of the mystic bond'' (*op. cit.,* p. 106). This objection would of course apply to the Masons more oppositely than to the modern Ku Klux Klan, which finds its staunchest supporters among those of the Fundamentalist persuasion.

To the opposition of the political idealist and the religious reformer of the Protestant type to secret societies must be added the historic antagonism of the Roman Catholic Church. This antagonism dates from the famous bull of Pope Clement XII in 1738 against Freemasonry, the first of a long series of fulminations of the Catholic Church against secret orders of all sorts. The attitude of the Catholic Church in this country towards se-

cret societies was formulated January 6, 1895, by
the Roman Catholic Archbishop of Cincinnati, apparently with the sanction of the Holy See. This
pronunciamento was directed primarily against
the Odd Fellows, the Knights of Pythias, and the
Sons of Temperance, but included all similar secret orders. They were condemned, first because
they tend to lead Catholics to Freemasonry which
is "under the absolute condemnation and excom-
munication of the Church" and indulges in a "Sa-
tanic warfare against everything Christian," secondly, because they "weaken a Catholic's regard
for the doctrines of the Church" and "inculcate
morality without the help of the Church," and,
thirdly, because Catholics who join these secret
orders tend to become "cool in their loyalty to
the Church."

The real basis of the opposition of the Catholic
Church to secret societies is suggested by the
Catholic writer, Rev. J. W. Book, in his little
work, *A Thousand and One Objections to Secret
Societies,* published in 1893 with the imprimatur
of the Church authorities. The book is cast in the
form of a dialogue between a priest and a young
man who seeks light on the question of joining
secret societies. The priest justifies the antagonism of his church to all secret societies and

especially oath-bound societies on the ground
that "by a divine right the Church has charge of
souls and consequently she has a right to know
what they are doing and *how* they are doing it.
But how can she judge of the lawfulness of an act
if it is not submitted to her judgment?" In other
words, it is a fundamental thesis of the philosophy
of the Roman Catholic Church that she is appointed by God to be the keeper of the consciences
of the faithful. There can be no secrets between
the individual and his spiritual guardian, the
Church.

On the whole, it can hardly be said that the
Catholic Church has been entirely consistent in
its attitude towards secret societies. It has re
fused to condemn the Knights of Labor and the
Grand Army of the Republic, both secret orders
with grips and passwords. It is of course obvious that any condemnation of these orders, especially the latter, would raise the ugly question as
to whether loyalty to the church should take precedence over loyalty to country, an issue which
American Catholics have as a rule studiously
avoided. There has been no serious opposition
to Catholic students' joining college fraternities.
Finally, it would appear that secrecy is condemned
not because of its inherent evils but because it

militates against the interest of the church. The famous Constitutions and special papal privileges enjoyed by the members of the Jesuit Order were kept secret, the members not being allowed to show these documents to outsiders. There were doubtless reasons of policy for this, such as the desire not to antagonize other non-secret Catholic orders that did not enjoy like papal privileges. To be sure, these secret documents have long since become public property, thanks to the suppression of the order and the seizure of its papers towards the close of the eighteenth century. But the fact remains that the church authorities did sanction its secret methods and later abolished the order mainly through the pressure of public sentiment. The order was revived by a bull of Pope Pius VII in 1814 and still exists.

Here, if anywhere, we are to find some slight justification for the bitter opposition of the Klan to the powerful Catholic secret society, the Knights of Columbus. The Klan's brutal accusations against this society are of course absurd. There is not the slightest ground for the belief that this order, whose Americanism is abundantly proven by its splendid war record, has ever lent its influence to concerted secret efforts, political or otherwise, inimical to the integrity of the nation's life. The charge of the Klan that the Knights of Columbus are seeking to subject America to the rule of the Pope is the sheerest nonsense. At the same time the memory of the secret activities of the famous Jesuit Order, revived by Pius VII in 1814 and still active, when taken in connection with the remarkable growth of the Knights of Columbus, the more or less secret character of this order and its avowed loyalty to the Holy Father and the Church, suffice to bring it constantly under the watchful and jealous eye of its Protestant rivals.

II

Towards the end of the nineteenth century the opposition to secret societies gradually waned. Fraternal organizations, largely secret, increased by leaps and bounds. Of some 568 fraternal orders in existence in 1900 only seventy-eight antedated the year 1880. Between the years 1880 and 1895, 490 of these fraternal orders arose. Any sketch of the social life of this nation to-day must give due importance to the fact that over seven percent of our population belongs to some fraternal order. These societies, six hundred and more in number, present a diversity of religious, political, racial and cultural elements in our civilization that is bewildering in its complexity. The secret society is no longer challenged as in the past on the ground that it is inimical to moral, religious, or political loyalties. Contrast, for example, the attitude towards the Freemasons in 1830 with the reception accorded the Shriners by the capital city of the nation June, 1923, when hundreds of thousands of members of this secret order preëmpted its streets and hotels and practically forced a suspension of the normal life of the city for a week. The citizens of Washington vied with each other in extending to the members of this secret society the utmost limits of their hospitality. On the wind-shields of their cars private citizens pasted the invitation "Hop in, Noble." The federal government gave to its employees a half-holiday that they might witness the Shriner parade. The secret societies have become important factors in American life. Great American cities compete for the honor of entertaining their conventions. The spirit of Wendell Phillips is to-day little more than a pious tradition.

Most remarkable has been the spread of the fraternal beneficiary societies, the godfather of which was Upchurch, a worker of Meadville, Pennsyl-

vania, who in 1868 organized the Ancient Order
of United Workmen and provided the model for
many later organizations. It is no accident that
these societies began their rapid rise about the
year 1880. For this year marks the dropping of
the frontier line from the census and the organization of the Standard Oil Trust, two facts indicating that America had made the transition from
the old individualistic pioneer democracy of earlier days to the highly centralized and interde-
pendent industrial society of the present, dominated by the big business corporation. The era
of "big business" bore especially hard upon the
wage-earning class. It was forced to arm itself
with protective measures in order to survive.
The fraternal beneficiary society, like the trades-
union, was created by this class to assure to itself
a more permanent status in the new order of
things. Secrecy, in so far as it is made use of by
these fraternal beneficiary societies, is little more
than a means of safeguarding members against
impostors and those who seek to exploit them.
Signs, grips, passwords, and the like secret paraphernalia obviously serve the useful purpose of
enabling members of these orders to identify each
other wherever they meet, thus assuring themselves that the aid given or the friendship ex-

tended is not abused. There is nothing in this
form of secrecy inimical to public welfare or in-
jurious to religion or morals. The secret features
are in fact subordinated to the socially valuable
ends for which the society is organized. Oaths,
in so far as they are used, are merely means for
inducing the individual member to live up to the
full measure of his responsibilities as delimited
by the purposes of the order.

Equally important, however, with the economic
benefits of the secret society is the rôle it has
played in the social life of America. To appreci-
ate what this rôle is we must remind ourselves
that the real texture of American social life is to
be found, not in the large cities with their welter
of racial groups nor in the great industrial centers, where the blue sky overhead and the daily
wage seem to be the only bonds that unite men,
but in the small town. The spirit of the small
town is writ large in the universal fondness for
picnics, circuses, parades, church socials, conventions, and secret societies. The small town mind
emerges in the amazing popularity of the moving
picture, essentially a small town amusement; in
the Ford, the small townsman's means of locomo-
tion; in revivals, the small town type of religion;
in Fundamentalism, small town theology; and in

the enthusiastic reception of Mr. Bryan's denunciation of evolution which fits the small town idea of science. Allusion has been made to the fact that the Klan is essentially a small town movement. It is such because the stronghold of the hundreds of secret lodges in this country is to be found in the small town. Every town and many villages have their lodge of the Odd Fellows, the Masons, the Loyal Order of the Moose, or the Elks. The smaller cities of the Southwest, which can seldom boast of a decent church or school building, not to mention a considerable library or an art gallery, are often the possessors of magnificent Masonic temples costing hundreds of thousands. It is worth while asking why the secret society plays such an important rôle in small town life, thereby becoming an integral part of the social fabric of the nation.

Life in the small town, as portrayed for us in Sinclair Lewis's *Main Street,* has lost the adventurousness, the creative individual initiative of pioneer days, and has become sicklied over with the deadly monotony of a conventionalized democracy. The democratic emphasis upon equality, publicity, and like-mindedness leaves whole phases of man's nature to starve. The drab humdrum of conventional democracy has no place for the mys-

tery men crave. It is more or less inimical to
those personal intimacies to be had only within
the exclusive circle of a favored group. It is utterly devoid of the pomp and circumstance or the
imaginative appeal of rank and noble blood. With
the very best of intentions democracy tends to
magnify mediocrity. Its god is the "average
man."

Those secret societies whose emphasis is primarily social, have arisen to meet these deficien-
cies of conventional democracy so strongly in evidence in the small town. They offer an element
of mystery lacking in the prosaic round of small
town life. The hocus-pocus of a secret ritual in-
troduces the dramatic note. Its absurdities are
lost upon the individual who feels that through
it he escapes into an Invisible Empire whose
secret ramifications reach to the utmost bounds
of the nation. High-flown titles and the mystic
alliterative appeal of grotesque neologisms such
as "Klud," "Klokard," "Klexter," "Kleagle,"
"Kloran," "Klavern," and the like tickle the
imagination and fascinate by their strangeness.
Gorgeous costumes provide color and variety.
The pomp of a parade along streets lined with
gaping villagers suggests a feeling of social importance and flatters the pride of the small town

mind. The fraternal convention with its march-
ings, its convivialities, its effusions of post-
prandial wit, its good fellowship and larger social
contacts, furnishes a most grateful means of escape from the tyranny of business and the deadly
monotony of small town life, providing something
like an Aristotelian katharsis of the starved emotions, when it does not degenerate, as is sometimes
the case, into a debauch.

In the fraternal orders in which the social note
predominates secrecy plays a most important rôle.
From the Masons, with their historic traditions
and their various subdivisions, down to the most
insignificant local order, all alike seek to intrigue
the imagination of the small town dweller with
their mystery. Secrecy is an inherent and indispensable part of their equipment, for without secrecy it would be vain to seek to escape the light
of the drab and commonplace democratic day.
The bar of secrecy makes possible a charmed land
of mystery and imagination and intimate friendships. It is a make-believe land to be sure, often
a cheap and tawdry substitute even for the unin-
teresting realities of small town existence. But
the barrier of secrecy gives to this land of make-
believe a fascinating charm. It even lends to it in
the minds of the initiated as well as of the

"aliens," as the Klan calls outsiders, a sort of supernal reality. Whatever takes place within this veil of secrecy assumes a unique importance. It makes friendships more genuine, wit more spontaneous, laughter more contagious. The moral banalities of the ritual, the absurd and ridiculous nomenclature of officers or the childish mummeries of the secret paraphernalia become interesting, dignified, even awe-inspiring. There still remains in all of us, despite "the wreckful siege of battling days," something of childhood's fondness for the wonderful land of make-believe.

Obviously the secrecy of the fraternal order whose chief emphasis is upon the social side is in no wise incompatible with civic duties and a healthful social order. Secrecy merely serves to heighten the social function of these societies by providing a valuable means of escape from domestic and business drudgery. The secret fraternal order has arisen to meet very real needs of American life. It is the product of that natural tendency of men, remarked by DeTocqueville, to "set up, close by the great political community, small private circles" which shall minister to the needs of a human nature neglected and starved by a conventional democratic society.

In the light of the foregoing sketch it is perhaps

possible to classify secret societies into three
groups according to the rôles they ascribe to
secrecy. In the first group would fall the fraternal
beneficiary societies so popular among the wage-
earning class. Secrecy in this group is merely a
protective measure. A second group would include
those large fraternal orders whose membership is
drawn from the well-to-do middle class. In this
group secrecy serves as a means of lending variety
and interest to our poverty-stricken American life.
To these two types of societies whose use of secrecy is harmless and therefore tolerated by public
sentiment must be added a third group, the militant oath-bound societies who make use of secrecy
in the performance of acts or the carrying out of
programs the scope of which is not limited to the
membership of the secret order but affects directly the welfare of society as a whole. The old
Ku Klux Klan of Reconstruction days, organized
to resist the tyranny of carpet-bag rule, the *Vehm-
gerichte* of Westphalia that arose in the Middle
Ages to check the anarchy threatened by the dissolution of the strong government of Charlemagne,
the *Carbonarii* of Naples who sought to throw off
the yoke of Napoleon, the *Mafia* of southern Italy
organized to resist the police and to protect the
smugglers, the *Clan-na-Gael*, an Irish secret so-

ciety organized to resist English tyranny and perpetuated to some extent in the lawless Molly Maguires of the Pennsylvania coal mines—all these are illustrations of the militant, oath-bound, secret society which makes use of secrecy to carry out policies of vital interest to society as a whole. It is a matter of some importance, therefore, to determine to which of these three groups the modern Ku Klux Klan belongs.

III

Owing primarily to the planless opportunism that has characterized the Klan from the very beginning we find it strikingly inconsistent in this matter of secrecy. Reference has already been made to the question put to the official head of the Klan, Emperor W. J. Simmons, by Representative Fess, a member of the committee appointed by Congress to investigate the Klan, "Is the purpose of this order anything like that of the Invisible Empire in Civil War times?" to which Emperor Simmons replied, "No, sir; we have no conditions existing now that would justify such a modus operandi. This is purely a fraternal and patriotic organization." This statement is patently at variance with other public utterances of Emperor

Simmons and with the inferences to be drawn from the official Klan literature.

Later the following colloquy took place between Emperor Simmons and Mr. Campbell, chairman of the investigating committee. *Mr. Campbell:* "The fact, however, is that the mask worn by the Klansman has been used to conceal those who have had any purpose to serve, good or bad, and that they have been able to conceal their identity from the public does not strike you as being a question that should have your attention as Imperial Wizard of the Invisible Empire, or that you should go into the question of whether or not it would promote the welfare of the Invisible Empire to remove the mask?" (Congressional English is often fearfully and wonderfully made. The writer transcribes it as it stands in the record.) *Mr. Simmons:* "I will state that there is a possible ground there, just as there are a good many other things that we now have under consideration in the development of this infant organization. . . ." *Mr. Campbell:* "Men of such high and noble purposes as Klansmen should not conceal their names from the public or their faces from the public. Do you not think that it would be a good thing to let the public know who these noble men are?" *Mr. Simmons:* "Yes, sir, certainly; and at the proper time the public is going to know." *Mr. Campbell:* "When are you planning that the public shall know who the Klansmen are?" *Mr. Simmons:* "That is in the development of our work. We are simply making the organization. We are perfecting it in its ritualistic casting, and, in a way, we are in a state of childhood. The matter of wearing the robe and mask is nothing more or less than a memorial, or it is done for monumental purposes." This was spoken October 17th, 1921. Over two years have elapsed and the mask has not been removed.

There is a very real reason why the Klan has not discarded its mask and robe. They are absolutely necessary for the carrying out of the program the Klan has set for itself. This fact is abundantly recognized by the Klan leaders themselves. In a contribution to Klan literature by Rev. Ben Bogard, a Baptist minister of Little Rock, Arkansas, who "has been a member of the K. K. K. from its beginning in Arkansas" and who "defies any one to deny his statements," this representative of the gospel of peace on earth and good will among men says, "Every Klansman is a sworn detective. He is instructed to keep both eyes open and his mouth shut." Rev. Bogard informs us, "The number of the Klan is not being accurately passed out to the public for the reason that its membership is secret and its number is secret and you are possibly associated every day with some Klansman who will never tell you he is a member. *The secrecy of the order is its chief power* [italics are the writer's]. If the membership were known it would be like publishing to the world who the detectives are. Any thief could go around a known detective.''

Here is a plain statement that the Klan is primarily a militant order and that secrecy is indispensable to the carrying out of its aims. Just as detective bureaus are organized to operate in secret against the criminals of the community, so the Klan is a self-constituted detective society in the community. There is this fundamental difference, however; detectives, whether employed by the state, or private individuals, are always subject to the control of the constituted authorities of the community. The Klan, however, is a law unto itself. It exerts its detective function apart from any check save the judgment of its members. We have here, obviously, a situation fraught with danger to the community. Detectives are under constant danger of violating the laws or infringing upon the rights of the individual. They are for that reason and because of their methods seldom held in the highest respect by the community. Many detectives are doubtless valuable public servants. So long as we have lawless members of society we shall in all probability be forced to use the methods of the detective to control them. But to adopt the methods of the detective in a secret oath-bound organization not employed by the state or municipality and operating with no other restraint than its own sense of what is right is an utterly anomalous and dangerous procedure in a free country. It is nothing more nor less than the proposal to adopt principles and methods within a peaceful and law-abiding community that are justifiable only in wartime or when we are forced to deal with individuals or groups that are avowedly lawless. Where such methods are used to any great extent by a large organization such as the Klan there is practically no limit to the extent to which it may become a source of demoralization in the community.

IV

That the Klan has exerted a demoralizing influence upon community and national life by virtue of its secret methods there can not be the slightest doubt. The evidence in support of this statement is simply overwhelming. In every city or community where the Klan is a force to be reckoned with one finds "leading citizens" who will express frankly in private their opposition to the Klan but who close these interviews almost invariably with the words, "I prefer not to be quoted in this matter." A correspondent from Raleigh, North Carolina, states that while the Klan was condemned by the governor and stringent bills were introduced against it in the Senate and the House, "yet the acts finally passed were weak and ineffective. Many members seemed to fear the incalculable influence of the unknown members of the secret order among their constituents." A citizen of Atlanta states, "I find that among those men I know well and with whom I am at liberty to talk, the organization is a good deal of a joke. They are willing to laugh about it in private, but to be perfectly frank about it most of us would rather keep our mouths shut publicly." An educator in Alabama says, "I am bitterly opposed to the idea of the secrecy of the Klan and consider it cowardly to go around masked and ashamed to own its identity. . . . I think that many hold the same views as I do but because of its secrecy they do not care to be too outspoken for fear of consequences in a business way." A correspondent from Denver, Colorado, writes that while two years ago the general attitude of the community was that of opposition to the Klan, "To-day it is doubtful. The Klan propaganda is secret and insidious. People begin to be cautious in expressing themselves—in itself a bad sign as the Klan is itself a moral issue."

Here is a matter of serious concern for all patriotic citizens who wish well for their community, their state, or their country. When we have a great movement under way, claiming as its purpose the punishment of the criminal, the maintenance of pure Americanism, the preservation of the sanctity of womanhood and a general censorship over the morals of the community and the nation, and when the leading men of the community representing its best brains and finest culture, owing to the secret and militant methods of this movement, dare not come out and say what they think about it, we have something very closely approximating terrorism. To be sure, the Klan strives for just this psychological effect upon the community. There are doubtless members of the order who will be pleased when they read the statements above. Such utterances are a tribute to the Klansman's power. They flatter his pride. But what is the price paid for this paralyzing of healthful public sentiment through intimidation? It engenders a moral atmosphere thoroughly inimical to free democratic institutions.

It is a hard saying and yet true that the Klan is a breeder of cowards. It breeds cowards both inside and outside the Klan. It breeds cowards outside the Klan because it takes courage to fight an antagonist who strikes in the dark. It breeds cowards within the Klan because it offers effective concealment for the small and spiteful spirit. It places a premium upon the bully and the sneak. President Weaver of Mercer University, Georgia, well says: "Those who desire to improve the conduct of their fellow men, wearing the ghostly garb of the Ku Klux Klan, using the whip or tar and feathers, will enjoy for a time the exultation which the underman can not conceal when for a brief period he feels himself to be the possessor of power and the creator of fear." There is an element of this type of character in every one of us. It is particularly strong in the man of narrow outlook on life who chafes under a sense of his own insignificance and grasps eagerly at the mask and robe as a means of gratifying wounded pride or cowardly spite. For the Klan, in spite of its lofty claims and its best intentions, places in the position of power and initiative in the community the inferior man of limited intelligence, with strong prejudices, with fixed and unreasoning convictions upon politics, religion, or conventional morals. The Klan makes him supreme because it provides him with a mask, with cow-hide and tar-pot and the mysterious arm of an Invisible Empire, as a means of enforcing his own will and of closing the mouths of the real leaders of the community. The Klan in this sense is perhaps the most striking example this generation has furnished of the tyranny of the conventionally patriotic, often well-meaning but small-minded, mediocre man.

Wherever the Klan has become a power in a community its secret and militant methods have eaten like an acid into the fabric of society, disintegrating loyalties, setting man against man, and paralyzing social and civic enthusiasms. Reference has been made to the situation, created by the Klan in the larger cities of Oregon, such as Portland and Astoria. The chambers of commerce lost members and influence because of dissensions introduced by the Klan. In other communities the American Legion was torn by factional fights centering around the Klan. The issue of the Klan introduced an atmosphere of sus-

picion and distrust even into the great fraternal
societies such as the Masons and the Odd Fellows.
Most lamentable of all was the effect of the Klan
upon the numerous small local neighborhood
clubs where groups gathered in the homes for social and civic purposes with no thought of religious or other differences. The secret and militant methods of the Klan created an atmosphere
of restraint and antagonism, thus described by a
close observer: "Invariably the time would come
when the hostess of the evening would receive the
regrets of one or two members who had never
before absented themselves. Over those who did
assemble would hang a pall of forced gaiety, punc-
tuated by embarrassing gaps in the customary
flow of bantering conversation. The luncheon or
supper hour would be rushed a trifle, in hopes of
relieving the strained atmosphere. Throughout
the meal the host and hostess would exert themselves to restore the lost gaiety, without avail.
The once harmonious group seemed now to be a
collection of misfits—the congeniality was gone.
Over their coffee and cigars the men talked in
monosyllables of the weather and other commonplace topics. Uppermost in the mind of each was
a vital subject of public concern, the Ku Klux
Klan, but it was never mentioned. Already sus-

picion and distrust were eating into the community.''

Ex-Senator LeRoy Percy of Greenville, Mississippi, in a remarkable address delivered April 23, 1923, to his fellow townsmen, an address that should be read by all Americans where the Klan is an issue, says: ''This thing has come into our midst, parting friends, sowing discord, dissension, and hatred where there was gentleness and love and friendship; disrupting churches, threatening civic societies, destroying the spirit of cooperation, and making man look with suspicion on man and wonder whether his neighbor is his friend or his secret enemy. You walk the street and you feel that you are standing among hostile people. Standing less than twelve months from the time when we gathered on this platform together, and looking back through a mist of hate that has arisen from this Klan business, like miasma from a morass, it is hard to visualize the town as it was a year ago, it is hard to call it back.'' All good men and true owe ex-Senator Percy and others like him a vast debt of gratitude that they are courageous and patriotic enough to stand up, at the risk often of personal danger, and condemn this un-American monstrosity.

Thanks to the mask and robe, thousands of patriotic and well-intentioned Americans are induced to engage in secret methods which amount to a complete denial of the principles of true Americanism. They are made to stultify themselves. In section four of his oath of allegiance, as given in the Kloran, the Klansman is made to say, "I swear that I will most zealously and valiantly shield and preserve by any and all means and methods the sacred constitutional rights and privileges of free public schools, free speech, free press, separation of church and state, liberty, white supremacy, just laws, and the pursuit of happiness against any encroachments of any nature by any person or persons, political party or parties, religious sect or people, native, naturalized or foreign, of any race, color, creed, lineage or tongue whatsoever." Surely language could go no further in superlative and tautological asseveration of loyalty to free American institutions. This secret and militant organization proposes by its secret methods to defend the "sacred constitutional rights" of free speech, free press, and freedom of religious belief! What could be more absurd? The grotesque robes and masks, mysterious fiery torches, cow-hides, and tar-pots manipulated behind masks, threatening anonymous letters, and all similar terrorizing agencies used by this secret oath-bound order to enforce its will upon individuals and communities are utterly incompatible with the Klansman's sworn loyalty to "sacred Constitutional rights" of Americans.

Section 2, Article 3 of the Constitution says, "The trial of all crimes, except in cases of impeachment, shall be by jury." It is perfectly obvious that this constitutional right of trial by jury even in the case of the vilest criminal and the most disreputable social outcast is incompatible with pronouncements upon the conduct of fellow-citizens made in secret conclave and executed under cover of masks or through other extra-legal means. "Whenever any association of individuals," says Judge William B. Sheppard, "on their own account undertake to restrain or prohibit these [constitutional] rights by threats or by secret demonstrations of power or by other intimidations, they are invading the rights of the citizen and violating the safeguards of constitutional government. When they meet together in conclave or otherwise for the purpose of depriving any citizen of his liberty to exercise his opinion lawfully or to do what is not denounced by statute, they are invading the rights of such citizens and depriving him of a privilege guaranteed by the Constitution. . . . Any person engaged in a conspiracy to deprive one of his constitutional rights may be prosecuted in a federal court.''

In the light of the foregoing analysis the conclusion is inevitable that the modern Ku Klux Klan, like its historic predecessor, the old Klan, belongs in the third group of anti-social secret societies. That is to say, the facts indicate that the modern Klan's secret methods are thoroughly un-American and dangerous and therefore merit the condemnation of all good citizens. The Klan, however, steadily refuses to unmask. It insists strenuously that the mask and robe are absolutely necessary not only for the execution of the Klan's aims but also for its very existence. On the Klan's own showing, therefore, it has to face the alternatives either of discarding the mask and perishing through the loss of the one thing that gives it significance or of clinging to the mask and secret militant methods, thereby giving rise to vigorous moral condemnation that must in time prove to be the Klan's undoing. This conclusion, it must be confessed, places the Klan in a rather unpleasant predicament. To make its secrecy harmless at the price of social ineptitude or to retain its present secret anti-social methods at the price of moral condemnation and elimination are not pleasant alternatives. These alternatives in-

evitably suggest the query, which doubtless the
reader has already put to himself, whether the
Klan has not been a huge mistake. The uniform
opinion of the best element in every community is
that the Klan has never had any real justification
for its existence. It has flourished by creating
false issues, by magnifying hates and prejudices
or by exploiting misguided loyalties. It can not
point to a single great constructive movement
which it has set on foot. Men do not gather grapes
of thorns nor figs of thistles.

INDEX

American Federation of Labor, resolution with regard to the Klan, 97.

American Protective Association, and Nativism, 131; its methods of propaganda, 138; forerunner of the Klan, 166 ff.

American Unity League, 159.

Americanism, "one hundred percent," meaning of, 126; definitions of, 144 ff.

Andrews, President, 137.

Anti-Catholicism, see Ch. VI. Simmons quoted on, 28; in the Middle West, 34; in Oregon, 45 ff.; and the Scotch-Irish, 100; and the post-war mind, 124 ff.; sources of, among Klansmen, 169 f.; how far justifiable, 202 ff.

Baker, Ray Stannard, 71.

Beach, H. A., 140.

Berkson, I. B., 149.

"Birth of a Nation," effects of, 71.

Bismarck, 189.

Bliss, Cornelius, 137.

Bogard, Rev. Ben, 228.

Book, Rev. J. W., 214.

Brosnahan, Rev. T., 198.

Bryan, W. J., 21, 101, 103, 105, 115, 220.

Burleson, Postmaster-General, 6.

"Cahenslyism," 182.

Calvin, John, 20.

Campbell, Chairman of House Rules Committee, 28, 227.

Carbonarii, 225.

Carpenter, Deacon Philo, 210.

Carroll, David, 171.

Catholic Americans, attitude towards the Klan, 159; friction with Protestants due to Klan, 160 f.; imperialistic ambitions of, 164 f.; original status of, 172 f.; rise of "Americanism" among, 177 f.; "Cahenslyism" and, 182; suppression of "Americanism" by Pope Leo XIII, 185 f.; injustice of the Klan towards, 187 f.; theocratic autocracy of papacy and, 191 f.; dual sovereignty of church and state and, 203 f.

Catholic World, the, 177.

Chicago Defender, the, 34.

Clan-na-Gael, 225.

Clarke, E. Y., 7, 8, 12, 13, 16, 18, 22, 41, 132.

Clement XII, 213.

Cleveland, Grover, 137.

Commercialism, in the Klan, 8.

Columbus (Ga.) *Enquirer-Sun*, 14.

Corbin, John, 150.

Daily Journal of Commerce, the, 59.

Dallas News, the, 14.

Darwin, Charles, 114, 115.

Desmond, Humphrey J., 161.

DeTocqueville, 172, 207.

Dickson, Harris, 56.

Duffus, R. L., 32.

Evolution, 105.

241

Printed in the United States
76663LV00004B/51